D1429926

Owning Your Journey

How to Successfully Navigate the Community College Experience

First Edition

HUNTER KEENEY AND SUZONNE H. CROCKETT
Lamar State College Orange

Bassim Hamadeh, CEO and Publisher
John Remington, Executive Editor
Gem Rabanera, Senior Project Editor
Jessica Rosa, Editorial Assistant
Casey Hands, Production Editor
Asfa Arshi, Graphic Design Assistant
Kylie Bartolome, Licensing Associate
Natalie Piccotti, Director of Marketing
Kassie Graves, Vice President of Editorial
Jamie Giganti, Director of Academic Publishing

Copyright © 2023 by Cognella, Inc. All rights reserved. No part of this publication may be reprinted, reproduced, transmitted, or utilized in any form or by any electronic, mechanical, or other means, now known or hereafter invented, including photocopying, microfilming, and recording, or in any information retrieval system without the written permission of Cognella, Inc. For inquiries regarding permissions, translations, foreign rights, audio rights, and any other forms of reproduction, please contact the Cognella Licensing Department at rights@cognella.com.

Trademark Notice: Product or corporate names may be trademarks or registered trademarks and are used only for identification and explanation without intent to infringe.

Cover image: Copyright © 2021 iStockphoto LP/Drazen Zigic.

Printed in the United States of America.

Brief Contents

Table of Contents

Preface

The seed for writing *Owning Your Journey: How to Successfully Navigate the Community College Experience* was planted long ago, and it's a thrill (and a bit of a relief) to be writing the preface for it today. The project idea arose from our experiences in the community college student success arena, particularly through interaction with the remarkable young people we met along the way. Working with first-year students (who vary widely in terms of their ages, backgrounds, and dreams for their future) in the freshman seminar course is truly a humbling and inspiring exercise, and watching them overcome challenges and grow, academically and personally, is quite unlike any other teaching experience we've encountered. So when presented with the opportunity to tap into these experiences and undertake the writing of *Owning Your Journey*, the decision to pursue it was made with relative ease: we knew we had to jump.

This book was written for the first-year seminar or freshman student success course at the community college level. Our intention was to concisely address key issues for students in these courses as they begin their journey into the higher education experience. The first half of the text covers the basic characteristics of the community college environment, including the nature of the community college institution (Chapter 1); navigating admissions, advising, financial aid, and other college services (Chapter 2); prioritizing life activities for effective time management (Chapter 3); and learning to respectfully communicate and interact with peers and instructors on campus (Chapter 4). The last half of the book provides a practical and applicable approach to various topics including study techniques (Chapter 5); test-taking strategies (Chapter 6); online information literacy and using reference sources (Chapter 7); and, finally, preparing for graduation or transfer, and a rewarding career beyond the walls of academia (Chapter 8).

Owning Your Journey is written to speak directly to the student in an informal, relatable tone meant to enhance their engagement with and understanding of the book's content. It is intended to be approachable yet also convey the serious and challenging nature of the college experience. Although student-friendly, the chapters remain rooted in research literature and learning theory, and contain a wealth of practical strategies as well as frequent opportunities for personal reflection and peer collaboration. With eight succinct chapters, the book can easily be adapted to an 8-week course format or expanded into the traditional 16-week semester. There are multiple activities and review questions for each chapter, with ample space for the instructor to modify existing features or introduce their own assignments into the course.

Throughout the text, there is a strong emphasis on the critical importance of the student maintaining a positive mindset and a vision for their future. The overarching theme is one of self-exploration, encouraging the student to take ownership of their journey through developing self-confidence, a sense of personal accountability, and the sustained motivation needed to carry them through to a successful completion of their path.

CHAPTER 1

Setting Your Compass

Learning to Master Your Mindset and Planning to Succeed From Day One

Image 1.1

Introduction

The time has come, and you have arrived, my friend. Welcome to your journey! And what an exciting journey it truly is to navigate the higher education experience. The actions you take and practices you develop over the next few years will definitively shape your future trajectory and, hopefully, catapult you into a higher quality of life that you may already envision for yourself. If your path is still unclear, that's perfectly okay, too. What matters most at this stage is your general outlook and the quality of your intentions. Along these lines, this introductory chapter will focus on the following themes:

- Thinking positive and staying motivated throughout your academic experience
- Learning the community college landscape and considering your place within it
- Planning to succeed by envisioning your goals here at the start of your journey

Here's a brief summary of the main sections contained in Chapter 1. In "Mastering Your Mindset," the student is asked to consider the power of thinking positive and to look inward for personal motivation; the chapter includes Activity 1.1—What Drives You?—a reflective opportunity for students to identify personal factors that can drive them to stay motivated. "Meet Dr. K" invites the student to "meet" Dr. Hunter Keeney, as the textbook author shares a brief summary of his own educational and professional experience. "Community College by the Numbers" provides an overview of the community college landscape, including the nature of the institution, the students it serves, and a few standard measures for student success in this environment. And, finally, in "Beginning With the End In Mind," the chapter wraps up by asking the student to envision a successful outcome for themselves within the context of the community college experience.

I have learned over the years that when one's mind is made up, this diminishes fear; knowing what must be done does away with fear.

—Rosa Parks

Mastering Your Mindset

Welcome, fellow traveler! It is our distinct pleasure to greet you as you embark on one of the most pivotal, important, and enjoyable phases of your adult life—your college experience. Your initial thoughts on the difficulty of this journey are probably more or less accurate: college is not easy. But then, neither is anything that is truly worthy of your valuable time and effort. Higher education truly is an amazing experience, and you will find it is about much more than attending class, making good grades, and earning a degree. This will be a recurring theme in this text and (hopefully) throughout your academic career. And while it is certainly important to take your higher education experience seriously, the truth is there is nothing to fear. In fact, the key focus of this section of the chapter is about reducing fear and cultivating a positive mindset that will drive you to succeed and bring you greater happiness and fulfillment along the way. Stay tuned!

Now is probably a good time to mention that this textbook will almost certainly be unlike any other that you encounter throughout your college experience. Likewise, this course is not like any other, although it should apply to all of them. The first-year experience or freshman student success course is a personal endeavor, and as such, this book is written to speak directly to you, the student. This course is all about your experience and your journey. It is an opportunity to step back and reflect deeply on who you want to become and begin to manifest those thoughts into your reality. Of course, we will also cover a wealth of applicable knowledge and practical advice along the way to help you navigate the challenges of your college environment, but we will get to all that later. I am a firm believer that having a positive frame of mind, a sense of purpose, and an awareness of your situation and surrounding environment is of paramount importance and should be the primary consideration at this juncture.

Along these lines, the main focus of this introductory chapter is quite simple: think positive. It's time to become aware of why you are here and where you want to go, and to begin taking the first steps toward getting there. It's time to look inward and find the motivation that will carry you through to a successful completion of this part of your journey. In order to do this, it's necessary to learn the basics of mastering your mindset to prevent you from faltering too much along the way. The short list below outlines three key strategies to help out in this area. Each tip (or strategy) is then discussed in greater detail in the subsections that follow.

3 Tips for Mindset Mastery

1. **Stay Positive**
2. **Stay Motivated**
3. **Stay Present**

Stay Positive

Few things in life are more valuable than doing your best to keep a positive outlook about yourself, your life situation, and the world around you. Staying positive and happy will improve your relationships with others in every setting, including your college campus. Simply put, when you project positive energy in your life, good things will come back to you in return. There is even some evidence that suggests being positive may have academic benefits. Researchers at the Harvard Graduate School of Education found that happier students had higher GPAs and tended to be more motivated than their peers (Jones, 2015). Some studies have even found that being positive and happy is good for your overall physical health and well-being (Steptoe, 2019).

The benefits of staying positive are readily apparent and not difficult to understand. However, staying positive and just being happy in general can be challenging, particularly at certain times or situations in your life. It is no secret that anxiety can prevent us from having a positive mindset, and it is very common for students to be nervous and a bit overwhelmed entering any kind of college setting. It's okay—that is completely normal! Reducing this anxiety is the purpose of this chapter, and this entire textbook is meant as a "field guide" to help you build confidence, stay positive, and ultimately succeed on your journey. In order to help us stay positive and reduce anxiety, we need to get rid of the fear of the unknown, or at least learn to manage it. To do this, it's important to keep your purpose in mind.

One final note on staying positive involves your own reactions to unexpected situations along your academic path. If you get too attached in trying to control exactly how everything should happen, these little twists and turns can be very upsetting and will negatively impact your mindset. The truth is these little setbacks can be positive learning experiences that you can grow from. There is certainly great value in having a plan and overall vision for your future (more on this later), but it's also important to remember that how you react to situations as they occur in your life is equally valuable, if not more so. This concept applies to both your actions

Success Tip

Like Rosa Parks said in the opening quote, once you make up your mind to do something you know you must do, the fear surrounding this situation will go away. Remember that you are here to do great things and let that drive you. We will discuss this type of motivation further in the following subsection and in Activity 1.1, below.

and your emotional response and general state of mind—these are the things you *can* control. It's not always easy to remain calm and positive on your journey—in fact, sometimes it will seem impossible—but the truth is you always have a choice in how you react and respond to adverse situations. No one can ever take this from you.

Stay Motivated

Positivity and motivation are very closely related states of mind. That is, in order to stay positive, you need to stay motivated, and the opposite is also true. Both are extremely important, and in this subsection we'll discuss some aspects of motivation to help keep you, well ... motivated! Motivation begins with a sense of purpose and (you guessed it) a positive mindset. So the key question is, What motivates you? Why are you here and what do you wish to accomplish in two, five, or even 10 years? There are generally no wrong answers to these questions, and most of us have multiple reasons for what drove us to enroll in college in the first place and what will keep us going toward a successful conclusion.

These motivational reasons, or factors, are usually of a personal nature and very often involve family. You may feel pride (or pressure) based on the expectations of your family, which may have a strong tradition of college-going culture. On the other hand, you may take pride in being the first in your family to pursue the journey into higher education. You may be thinking more of yourself or your future family, for whom you'd like to set an example and provide a higher quality of life. Again, none of these are wrong and all can provide wonderful inspiration to keep you going on your path. Later, in Activity 1.1, we'll dive deeper into these personal motivational factors to identify and reflect upon the ones you believe will drive you the most to succeed. But first, we'll take a look at the final (and perhaps most slippery) mindset mastery tip in this section: spending time in the present moment.

Stay Present

This one is tricky, because in academic settings we are often required to live *in our heads*, recalling past bits of technical information or planning/anticipating future events—everything from next week's quiz to our eventual graduation and career beyond. Of course, this is all necessary to some degree to survive in the modern world, but excessive worry about the future or regret for the past is a recipe for stress and unhappiness. It is physically unhealthy and generally not conducive to mental clarity or a positive state of mind. Perhaps it's not really possible to *stay present* all the time, but taking a minute to breathe, quiet your mind, and silence that voice in your head (your ego) at various points in the day is well worth the effort.

This concept has been around for thousands of years and is rooted in Eastern traditions such as Buddhism, yoga, and various schools of meditation. It's what 1960s Harvard psychology professor turned spiritual guru Ram Dass famously articulated in his bestselling novel, *Be Here Now*. But the thing is, you don't need to be a master yogi or even practice formal meditation to benefit from this technique. It is available to everyone. Simply take a few minutes here and there to reflect and be grateful for where you're at in the present moment. Take a breath and pay attention to how you feel or just quietly observe your surroundings. You can do this at your house in the morning, on your commute to work or school, while studying or walking across campus, or even while taking an exam.

Try being present with others as well. Truly listen (without passing judgement) to your friend, classmate, instructor, or family member and give them your full attention. Learning this simple trick and remembering to do it can enrich your relationship with yourself and others and enhance your overall life experiences including higher education. It can reduce stress and anxiety and make things we may typically label unpleasant—waiting in traffic, doing housework, studying, doing homework, et cetera—much more productive and tolerable, even enjoyable. It's understandable that some readers may be a bit skeptical of this subtle strategy, but don't be afraid to give it a try! The results just might surprise you.

Activity 1.1 *What Drives You?*

In wrapping up this section, let's take a moment to consider mindset mastery Tip 2 (Stay Motivated) and reflect on what exactly drives us to enter the higher education arena and what may encourage us to stay motivated throughout the college experience.

On a separate sheet of paper, list the top three factors that serve as personal motivators for entering and completing college (this is wide open; it can be people in your life, personal ambitions or interests, financial or quality of life incentives, etc.). Then, explain your reasoning in four to five sentences (approximately 100 words) for each factor. You may discuss things such as why these factors are important to you, how they came to be important, and how or why you feel they will help motivate you toward academic success.

Meet Dr. K

Before we go any further, I feel a more personal introduction is in order. My name is Hunter Keeney, better known as "Dr. K" to the hundreds of students I've had the pleasure of meeting and working with over the years. I am the primary author of this text, but I certainly did not travel alone: my friend, colleague, and co-pilot, Dr. Suzonne Crockett, is very much on board. Her influence and experiences are embedded throughout these pages, and later on you will hear directly from her regarding her own remarkable journey that began right here at the community college.

My own college experience began with a deafening thud. To put it bluntly, I was a bad student. (Probably not what you'd expect to hear from the guy writing a book on student success, but it's true, nonetheless.) I was uncertain, unmotivated, a terrible procrastinator, and generally unskilled at managing the level of independence that comes along with life after high school. Overall, I was having a good time, and there's nothing wrong with that, in particular. But my lack of discipline and inability to balance my personal life with a commitment to my education was beginning to show, especially in my GPA. I took courses. I retook courses. I studied some and casually attended class but hung out with my friends more. For the first year or so of my college experience, you were more likely to find me in or around the student

(*Continued*)

Meet Dr. K (*Continued*)

center rather than in the class I had signed up for. I was enjoying my time but also causing myself a lot of stress and digging a hole that might have proved inescapable. In a nutshell, I was just barely scraping by. My technique for approaching college (or lack thereof) just wasn't working out and I was heading rapidly down a path to failure and disappointment.

And, yet, some 15 years later, there I was completing my doctoral degree in educational leadership with a 4.0 GPA in the program. I was named an Outstanding Doctoral Student by the university and earned a Professional Excellence award at work due to the publication of my doctoral research. At this point, I had already been teaching for five years and was applying for a tenured professor position at the college. Shortly after graduating, for the last time—finally, I took on an administrative role in the research department at my institution and continued teaching nearly a full load of classes. In my mind, I had made it, and in many ways I had. I am still proud of what I was able to overcome and accomplish, but the truth is, my journey wasn't over. It still isn't.

So how did I get from point A to point B? How did I go from a disorganized, undisciplined, struggling college student to a doctoral scholar, published researcher, and academic professional? Why does this matter? I am certainly not telling you all this to "blow my own horn" or attempt to impress you in any way. I'm telling you this because it's important to understand that most journeys do not proceed in a straight line. Sometimes not even close. You will experience some setbacks. That's okay. You may dramatically change your mind, or major, and decide to head in a completely different direction. That, too, is okay. It might take you longer than expected to get to where you want to go due to various life situations, some of which may be completely out of your control. All of this is okay. What matters most is to keep your attention, and intentions, set on the things that you can control—this is the overarching theme of this introductory chapter.

I sincerely hope you enjoy reading this book as much as we enjoyed writing it. Even more so, I hope it provides a road map and awakens within you the confidence and drive to succeed on your academic pathway and beyond. All the best on your journey!

—Dr. K

Community College by the Numbers

The term *community college* is used most frequently in this book, and in research and academic literature, to describe any two-year college institution, including those that may alternatively be called "junior" or "state" colleges in many cases. For the sake of consistency, convention, and simplicity, we will most often stick with the term *community college* when referring to all institutions in this broad and diverse category. In this section, we'll take a look at the community college institution itself, including its history and general characteristics, the students it serves (aka you and your peers), and what we currently know about prospects for success in this academic establishment. Since you are now a valued member of this establishment, it's a good time to explore the nature of where you're at and who you are here with in order to maximize your chances for success.

The Institution

A **community college** can be defined as any two-year institution that provides higher education and training for students who intend to earn a specialized award or certificate, as well as those seeking transfer to a traditional four-year university. Although not as old as the university system, these institutions have been a part of the higher education landscape for over 100 years and have swelled in number since their origin. The first community college was established in 1901 as a junior college branch of the University of Chicago, and today, there are approximately 1,050 community college institutions operating in the United States alone (American Association of Community Colleges, 2022). The majority of these institutions are publicly funded, and some are quite large. The Lone Star College System in Houston, Texas, serves over 73,000 students, making it the highest enrolled two-year campus in the nation; it ranks sixth in enrollment for *all* colleges in the United States, including universities (National Center for Education Statistics, 2020).

In general, though, community colleges are typically smaller in size, enabling them to provide a more intimate and student-centric educational experience compared to most four-year institutions. Average class sizes at the community college range from 25–35 students, whereas some introductory-level courses at a university may contain 300 students or more (Riskey, 2021). This means that students in the community college classroom usually have more direct access to their professors—who, in turn, are able to focus more on teaching and are far less burdened by the university demands of research, publication, and tenure.

In addition to size, another prominent feature of the community college is the cost of attendance. Specifically, the low cost of attendance. According to College Board (2021), the average yearly tuition and fee total for public two-year colleges is $3,440. This is less than half the cost of a public four-year college, which averages over $9,400 a year for in-state students. Out-of-state students at the university fork over nearly $24,000 per year, and the average annual cost of a private four-year college is over $32,000 (College Board, 2021)! Even with the lower cost, community college students still utilize various resources to help out with expenses. Nearly 60% of all community college students receive some kind of financial aid, the most common type being federal Pell grants, which do not require any form of repayment by the student (American Association of Community Colleges, 2022).

One final note on the community college as an institution involves the ease of acceptance and admission. The majority of two-year colleges are intended to be largely open to the public and most of these have very few admissions requirements beyond providing a high school diploma (or GED) and completing the application process. For this reason, they are sometimes referred to as "open admissions" institutions. In a recent study, Community College Review (2022) found the national average acceptance rate for all community colleges to be 79%, with the public community college rate being slightly higher at 86%. Contrast this with an average acceptance rate of about 70% for universities (Kowarski, 2021). This is one of several reasons why many students start at a community college to gain some traction and experience before transferring to the university. And while most four-year colleges do accept the majority of students who apply, it's interesting to note the admission prospects at the elite Ivy League institutions on the far other end of the spectrum. For example, acceptance rates at Harvard (3.4%), Columbia

University (3.7%), and Princeton (4%) all represented record-breaking low numbers in 2021, fueled by a national surge of applicants during the COVID-19 pandemic (Paramita, 2021). Such intense competition has led to instances of widespread cheating and scamming to get children of the rich and famous into top-tier institutions, as portrayed in the popular 2021 Netflix documentary film *Operation Varsity Blues: The College Admissions Scandal.*

The Students

The American Association of Community Colleges (AACC) recently published a summary of statistical data painting an informative picture of the community college student population. The AACC (2022) found that there are approximately 6.2 million students currently enrolled in U.S. community colleges, plus an additional five million taking noncredit courses. The number of community college students attending for credit (6.2 million) represents approximately 60% of all college students, nationwide: approximately 10.3 million in total (American Association of Community Colleges, 2022). More than two million community college students are currently taking at least one course online, and this trend has been growing steadily over the years (National Center for Education Statistics, 2021a).

The AACC study revealed that the majority of these two-year students (57%) are female in gender, and the ethnic demographics break out approximately as follows: 27% Hispanic, 13% African American, 44% White, 6% Asian/Pacific Islander, 1% Native American, and the remaining 9% composed of mixed race, unknown, and nonresident (American Association of Community Colleges, 2022). Interestingly, the National Center for Education Statistics (2010) reports that female college enrollment (for all undergraduate institutions) surpassed male enrollment in 1980, and it appears the gap has continued to widen. In fact, women now constitute nearly 60% of all college enrollment in the country (National Center for Education Statistics, 2021b). And although there has been enrollment growth in all races, the percentage of minority students has steadily increased, meaning the corresponding proportion of White students has declined. This makes the college enrollment trend somewhat like a microcosm, mirroring the trajectory of the U.S. population as a whole: toward greater diversity.

We know that the community college student population is slightly older, on average, than that of the traditional four-year university, which means these students are more likely to be juggling the demands of parental responsibilities and work life. This factor likely accounts for the 65% of two-year students who attend part time (American Association of Community Colleges, 2022), perhaps unable to commit to a full load of courses in many cases.

Furthermore, statistics show that nearly 30% of community college students are classified as **first generation**, which means that neither of a student's parents earned a bachelor's degree or higher. Many of you reading this right now may find yourself in this category. If so, why not wear this designation as a badge of honor? After all, these individuals are breaking new ground and setting patterns that can positively affect not only themselves but also

Author's Note

If you can take a full load of classes, there are good reasons to consider doing it. Full-time students are statistically more likely to persist and tend to be more successful in general at the community college—see next section.

generations that follow as their family trees branch out and expand through time. Many institutions around the country directly acknowledge and celebrate their "first gen" students through staff-supported publicity campaigns or other forms of recognition to show appreciation for this unique population.

In addition to a large first-generation population, community colleges also tend to serve a greater proportion of minority and low-income students compared to a university (Community College Research Center, 2022). Furthermore, many community college students face unique challenges in their educational experience. About 60% reportedly take one or more remedial courses within their first three years of college (Community College Research Center, 2022) and nearly one in five report some type of learning or physical disability (American Association of Community Colleges, 2022). Despite these challenges, many thousands of students like you go on to successful degree completion or transfer, as detailed in the following section.

Measures of Success

Success in the community college can mean different things for different people, but in general the ultimate goals are usually to graduate with some type of credential and/or transfer to a four-year university. Two-year institutions provide opportunities to earn a dizzying array of certificates and other awards—some are now even approved to grant bachelor's degrees—but the most common award is the two-year associate degree. In academic year 2019 (fall 2019 through summer 2020), community colleges awarded some 865,504 associate degrees, over 599,397 certificates, and approximately 21,350 bachelor's degrees (American Association for Community Colleges, 2022). These are impressive numbers to be sure, and any of these roughly 1.5 million awards can certainly be life-changing events for the recipients. However, it's also important to be aware that many students never complete their journey and earn one of these valued certificates or degrees. Statistics show that the average community college graduation rate is about 25% (American Association for Community Colleges, 2022), meaning only one in four students complete their associate degree within three years of their first semester. Nearly 60% of community college students will finish an associate degree within six years but, unfortunately, most of the remaining 40% will never graduate (American Association for Community Colleges, 2022).

Another common measure for college success is student retention or persistence. These terms mean essentially the same thing: that the student stays enrolled at the institution. Of course, you have to remain enrolled in order to complete, so there is generally a direct and positive relationship between student retention and graduation rates—that is, as retention rates go up, graduation rates tend to increase as well. The standard metric for retention is the one-year retention rate, which is usually measured from the beginning of one fall semester to the next since this is the semester in which most first-time students begin their academic career. Using this standard time frame, **student retention** can be defined as the percentage of students from a fall semester that are still enrolled at the institution one year later. The Community College Research Center (CCRC) found that one-year retention rates at public two-year colleges currently average just under 60% (2022). This means that nearly 40% of students that enter college in a given Fall semester are no longer enrolled by the next Fall. As mentioned in the author's note above, attending full-time versus part-time appears to play a role in student success with regard to this metric. The retention rate for full-time students stands at around 70% whereas less than half (46%) of all part-time students will return to campus the following Fall semester (Community College Research Center, 2022).

Although there are many others out there, the final success measure we will cover in this section is transfer to a four-year college or university. For many community college students, this is the primary goal of attending the two-year college (although it never hurts to complete a certificate or associate degree in the process). According to a recent publication by the National Student Clearinghouse Research Center (2021), 31% of the community college students in the study had transferred to a four-year institution within six years, even though about 80% of them indicated in their first semester that they intended to earn a bachelor's degree or higher. Of the total original cohort of students, only about 15% earned a bachelor's degree within six years, and the study found that transfer students who enrolled full time were significantly more likely to attain this degree compared to those who enrolled part time. This same study found that close to half (42%) of the students who successfully transferred to four-year colleges had earned an associate degree or certificate prior to transfer.

Beginning With the End in Mind

As we wrap up the chapter in this final section, it's a good time to reflect and focus on where you are and what lies ahead of you. First off, do not be alarmed by the statistics in the previous section! They are certainly not meant to induce fear or panic. Rather, it's important to be aware of the setting you're in and the average odds for success so that you can understand and overcome the adversities that prevent many students from successfully completing their journey.

The important thing to remember is you are not average, nor are you defined or controlled by your situation. For example, recall that most community college students attend part time, many of them having no choice due to various demands in their daily lives. Many others have learning disabilities to manage or may come from a first-generation home where there is little to no direct experience with higher education. Despite these odds, the encouraging truth is that millions of these students have successfully navigated their community college experience and then gone on to bigger and better things in their lives. Every individual's experience is uniquely their own and all have the potential to achieve. By starting out with the mindset of staying positive, staying motivated, and staying present, you are well on your way to bringing your own personal vision of success to life.

So what does success look like to you? Can you see it yet? Most everyone in your position considers graduation and/or transfer as a major component of their academic success. That is certainly a good place to start. Do you plan to go for your bachelor's or even earn a master's or doctoral degree? Do you want to work in health care, education, the arts, or computer science, or start your own business? Perhaps you simply want to make your family proud by being the first member to earn a college certificate or degree. Do you aspire to do something about which you are truly passionate and make a difference in the lives of those around you?

Whatever it is you are dreaming of doing, *now* is the time to get excited about it! Picture yourself already achieving any stage of your success, even if your path is not completely clear at the moment. In other words, begin with the end in mind. Be proud of yourself for being here and have confidence that if you use this technique along with the previous mindset mastery strategies, you can build a solid foundation that can absolutely carry you to wherever you want to go. Right now, you are in the community college and that is a wonderful place to start.

End-of-Chapter Questions

1. **Recall.** What is a first-generation student, and do you find yourself in this category? Define retention rate and give the average retention rate for community colleges.
2. **Engage.** Share your reflection from Activity 1.1 with another student in the class. Discuss with each other any common ground or differences you may have regarding your motivational factors, then document any feedback or response received from the other person.
3. **Reflect.** Consider the three tips for mindset mastery. Which one do you think may be most difficult for you? Discuss any difficulties in your life that may negatively affect your ability to stay positive, motivated, or present, and provide some possible solutions to overcome these difficulties based on your own ideas or information provided in the chapter.
4. **Create.** Let's get your game plan on paper! Write out your academic goals for this semester, one year from now, two years from now, and three years from now. Be sure to discuss some of the practices and the dedication you believe it will take to achieve these goals. As we mentioned in the chapter, it's okay if things don't go exactly as planned, but it's still good to have a vision and some overarching goals for yourself. The time to get excited about your journey is now!

References

American Association of Community Colleges. (2022). *Fast facts 2022.* https://www.aacc.nche.edu/wp-content/uploads/2022/05/AACC_2022_Fact_Sheet-Rev-5-11-22.pdf

College Board. (2021). *College costs: FAQs.* https://bigfuture.collegeboard.org/pay-for-college/college-costs/college-costs-faqs

Community College Research Center. (2022). *Community college FAQs.* https://ccrc.tc.columbia.edu/community-college-faqs.html

Community College Review. (2022). *Average community college acceptance rate.* https://www.communitycollegereview.com/acceptance-rate-stats/national-data

Jones, V. (2015, March 26). *Because I'm happy: An intriguing study notes a correlation between a student's level of happiness and GPA.* Usable Knowledge, Harvard Graduate School of Education. https://www.gse.harvard.edu/news/uk/15/03/because-i%E2%80%99m-happy

Kowarski, I. (2021, November 9). 11 colleges with the lowest acceptance rates. *U.S. News and World Report.* https://www.usnews.com/education/best-colleges/the-short-list-college/articles/colleges-with-the-lowest-acceptance-rates

National Center for Education Statistics. (2010, July). *Status and trends in the education of racial and ethnic minorities.* https://nces.ed.gov/pubs2010/2010015/indicator6_24.asp

National Center for Education Statistics. (2020, April). *Digest of education statistics.* https://nces.ed.gov/programs/digest/d19/tables/dt19_312.10.asp

National Center for Education Statistics. (2021a, January). *Digest of education statistics.* https://nces.ed.gov/programs/digest/d20/tables/dt20_311.15.asp

National Center for Education Statistics. (2021b, March). *Digest of education statistics.* https://nces.ed.gov/programs/digest/d20/tables/dt20_301.10.asp?current=yes

National Student Clearinghouse Research Center. (2021, September 23). *Tracking transfer.* https://nscresearchcenter.org/tracking-transfer/

Paramita, P. (2021, April 8). 2021 college acceptance rates: The latest admissions trends [Blog post]. *InGenuis Prep.* https://ingeniusprep.com/blog/2021-college-acceptance-rates/

Riskey, E. (2021, August). *Community college vs. university: The big differences.* Study.com. https://study.com/blog/community-college-vs-university-the-big-differences.html

Steptoe, A. (2019). Happiness and health. *Annual Review of Public Health, 40*, 339–359. https://www.annualreviews.org/doi/10.1146/annurev-publhealth-040218-044150

Image Credits

IMG 1.1: Copyright © 2015 Depositphotos/happyalex.

CHAPTER 2

Scanning Your Horizons

Getting to Know Your Campus and the Services It Has to Offer

Image 2.1

Introduction

Now that you are on campus, it's time to get to know your surroundings—the people, places, and services that are there for your benefit. This chapter focuses on connecting with the key student services you will encounter upon your entry into the community college environment. As such, the main emphasis will be on the offices of admissions, advising, and financial aid, since they will be the most crucial services for getting you in the door and onto your academic pathway. At the end of the chapter, we will also take a broader view and explore a variety of other offices and services you are likely to have available on your campus. Chapter 2 will focus on the following themes:

- Getting familiar with admissions and advising and the valuable services they provide

- Knowing your financial aid office procedures and the details of different types of aid that are available
- Taking a broader look at your campus and several of the various other offices and services that can work to your educational advantage

Here's a brief summary of the main sections contained in Chapter 2: In "First Contacts: Admissions and Advising," the offices responsible for getting students into college and into the classroom are explored, including the basic process of college application and how students can benefit from academic advising. This section includes Activity 2.1—Crafting Questions for Your Advisor, in which students will create a list of questions regarding their academic future that they would ask in an advising session. "Financial Aid Demystified" describes the various types of local and federal aid available for students and covers the basic process for applying for financial aid. The differences between aid types and the dangers of excessive student loan debt are also discussed. "The Grand Tour: A Bird's Eye View of Your Campus" provides students an opportunity to broaden their campus perspective and survey other offices and services their college is likely to provide via Activity 2.2—Virtual Campus Tour.

A dream is the bearer of a new possibility, the enlarged horizon, the great hope.

—Howard Thurman

MEET DR. CROCKETT

By around my third-grade year, I already knew I wanted to become a teacher. I was not the sharpest crayon in the box, but my caring parents always taught me that even broken crayons still colored and could work just as well as all the other crayons.

My academic journey was not an easy one. In the ninth grade, I failed algebra. But rather than letting that break me, I went on to become a certified math teacher, and my first teaching assignment was—you guessed it—Algebra I: the very course I failed as a young adult. I was a developmental mathematics student in college and now I teach math and have a doctorate in developmental education administration. Some might say I take lemons and make lemonade.

My journey in higher education has been incredible, and it all started at the community college. I found my home in places like the tutoring center on campus. This was one of the student-centered services we will explore in this chapter; they will be crucial to your success! Over time, study skills and time management became my allies, and so began my successful journey to achieving my associate degree, my bachelor's degree, my master's degree, and finally my doctoral degree. I learned how to become a successful student because I realized that the race for education is not given to the swift (those who learn easy) nor the strong (those who are naturally smart), but it is given to those who endure (study and work hard) until the end.

No, I was not born with study skills; I worked to achieve them. I was not a traditional college student, but I was married to a loving husband who always supported my dream of higher education (thank you, Ronnie). I also have four wonderful children (Susan, Millicent, Ronnie Jr., and Clarence) who inspired me to

(Continued)

MEET DR. CROCKETT (*Continued*)

be a mom with a degree. You see, I could not tell my children about the value of higher education and not have a degree of my own to back it up.

I hope you got a sense of my amazing journey of using knowledge and skills that you will obtain from this course. Learn to use these tools to your advantage and your road will also lead to success!

First Contacts: Admissions and Advising

The admissions and advising departments typically work hand in hand in their mission to get students in the doors of the community college and into the classrooms where they need to be. High-quality services departments may even provide a little encouragement and motivation in the process. It's worth noting that all of the different departments we will discuss in this chapter generally fall under the umbrella of what we call student services, in higher education. This aptly named collection of departments is focused on serving you, the student, and understanding how they function and what they have to offer can greatly enhance your academic and student life experience in multiple ways. We'll begin with an overview of what is generally your very first point of contact: the admissions department. Although the majority of you reading this are likely already admitted, there is value in understanding the elements of this procedure. For instance, in the event that you transfer to another institution, you will have to repeat this same basic process, so a brief review can't hurt.

Admissions

As we discussed in Chapter 1, the process of gaining admission into community colleges is typically not as complex or restrictive compared to most universities. This certainly works in the student's favor, as you will probably not need to worry about scoring high on a standardized test or entrance exam, being at the top of your high school class, or writing a persuasive application letter to plead your case for admission, as is required by many four-year institutions. In fact, the majority of public community colleges have open admissions policies (U.S. Department of Education, 2017), as they are intended to grant the general public affordable access to a two-year associate degree and the opportunity for university transfer.

Although technically the only requirement for entry into an open admissions (or open enrollment) institution is a high school diploma or GED, very few open admissions institutions have 100% acceptance rates. This is because students neglect to complete one of the required elements of the admissions process by the specified date. In addition to providing a high school transcript, diploma, or GED, here is a list of common items that must be completed or provided in order to complete the application process and gain full admission into the college:

- A completed application form
- Application fee (sometimes required)

- Placement tests in math and English usually must be taken
- A driver's license or proof of ID is required

In some cases, additional documentation or proof of English proficiency may be necessary for international students. Also, depending on the institution, it may be necessary to attend orientation or acquire a student ID or parking pass before you can see your advisor and register for classes. So what's the bottom line? Make sure you know all the required elements of the application process at your college and get them checked off as soon as you can. The sooner you get in the door and see your advisor, the sooner you can get registered for the classes you want. Many classes, or class times, can be highly sought after by your fellow students and may not be available as the first day of the term draws near. In fact, some will fill up weeks in advance of the semester start date.

Success Tip

When in doubt, contact your admissions department! Even if you think you are clear on all the requirements, a quick email or phone call can ensure you are on the right path. These professionals are there to help you gain admission to the college and they're more than happy to do just that.

Advising

After your first contact in the admissions office, the next stepping-stone on your path to the classroom is the advising department. Academic advising is crucial to getting you on the right path for your educational goals and making sure that you stay the course. Depending on your institution and your academic standing, you may end up in multiple advising sessions, possibly even before every semester you attend. This is a positive benefit for you because a good advisor will know which courses you should take for your program, when they are offered, the sequence in which they should be taken, and any prerequisites that may be required. In fact, it is not uncommon to sit down and map out your entire two-year course sequence plan for obtaining your degree in your very first meeting. *This* is what we mean by having an overall vision for your educational goals! And it really is exciting (and motivating) to see it mapped out on paper in front of you.

Beyond the encouraging personal stories and accounts from students, academic advising is also recognized as a growing field in educational research. And, overall, the results are looking good. One study found a significant positive relationship between academic advising and student satisfaction and success (Young-Jones et al., 2013). The majority of students in this case felt empowered by their advisors and walked away with a greater sense of responsibility for their own education and increased confidence in their academic abilities. Others have suggested that academic advisors play a key role in speeding up the major selection process, improving student retention, and keeping students on a timely path to graduation (Thomas, 2017). Advisors are in a unique position to provide students with a consistent relationship on campus, giving them a chance to regularly communicate with someone who cares about their success. In this way, advisors are able to fill a long-term supportive role whereas some faculty often are not, due to other demands on their time.

With any luck, you will develop a consistent, positive relationship with an advisor who can be a combination of ally, supporter, mentor, and friend. Something to consider in the student-advisor relationship is the expectations of both parties during an actual advising session. What do you both expect to gain and accomplish in such a meeting? For instance, you may have certain questions for them; they will certainly have questions for you. It is not uncommon for both student and advisor to prepare certain questions beforehand so that the session is more productive and enjoyable. With that in mind, prior to your actual meeting together, consider the following questions your advisor may ask you to address:

- What is your current or expected major here at the college?
- If undecided, what are your interests or the possible majors you are considering?
- Do you have any prior experience at this college or any other?
- Which areas do you consider to be your strengths as a student (reading, writing, math, science, etc.)?
- Which areas do you anticipate may be more challenging for you as a student?
- When do you wish to graduate?
- Do you plan to transfer, and if so, where?

This is just a small sample, but definitely something to consider before your next appointment. In fact, let's do a quick thought experiment. Really quick. Take two minutes and jot down the answers to the questions above, just to see if you would be prepared. Time yourself (two minutes or less); we'll wait ... All done? Nice! If you knocked these out in two minutes or less, congrats! You already have a pretty good idea about yourself and where you are heading, academically. If you weren't quite certain on some of the answers, that's okay, too. In fact, if you hesitated a bit or struggled to complete these in the short time allotted, I have some good news for you: that's where your advisor comes in! They have the knowledge and experience to help you answer big questions just like these and get you on a solid path to your future.

Activity 2.1 *Crafting Questions for Your Advisor*

Okay, that was fun, but now it's your turn to ask the questions. Surely you have questions in your mind about your immediate and long-term educational future. You may be wondering what to take next semester, how to choose the right major, how to get into a certain program, et cetera.

On a separate sheet of paper or in the space provided below, list at least five questions that you would like to ask your advising professional if they were sitting across from you right now. Make them as specific to your educational program or interests as possible. When you are finished, hold on to these! They may come in handy the next time you find yourself in the advising office.

1.

(Continued)

Activity 2.1 *(Continued)*

2.

3.

4.

5.

Financial Aid Demystified

College graduates with a bachelor's degree typically earn some 66% more than those with only a high school diploma (approximately $1 million more over a lifetime), and more jobs than ever require a college education to get in the door (National Center for Education Statistics, 2022a). These eye-popping statistics seem favorable for future college grads, and it appears that getting a postsecondary credential will become increasingly important to compete in the job market of tomorrow. Despite these growing demands to attend and complete college, there remains a major barrier to higher education attainment for many people: the cost. Even with the expansion of the Pell Grant and other forms of aid, the inescapable truth is that college is simply more expensive today than ever before. Of course, there are some exceptions to this trend, and you are most likely to find them—yep—at the community college. Recently, some two-year schools have been able to actually reduce tuition or even waive it altogether in some cases, although this is not very common.

Even if you are lucky enough to find yourself at one of these lower cost institutions, chances are you are still paying enough tuition, fees, and other costs to put you outside of your financial comfort zone. If so, you are most certainly not alone. In a recent survey of over 10,000 students from across the country, over half (56%) reported they were unable to afford tuition post-COVID-19 and were considering other financing options or leaving college altogether to seek full-time employment (OneClass, 2020). Clearly, we are entering an age where exploring your options for affording your college experience is of the utmost importance. If you know what is out there and where to look, you may be surprised by how many options you actually have. Without a doubt, the best place to begin asking questions and getting the help you need is at your school's office of financial aid. Let's take a look at some general options and the overall process for getting financial assistance to keep you in the classroom, working toward your goals.

Local Financial Aid Options

There are a lot of financial aid options out there and every institution will have its own unique array of aid available to you. Let's start local. Before jumping straight into federal assistance (although we will very soon), check into your immediate surroundings to see what options you may have that could be easier to acquire and may not require repayment. Several local aid options to explore may include the following:

- Scholarships
- Institutional aid
- Work-study programs
- State aid

Scholarships are a great option to explore and may be offered by the college itself or by some local entity looking to promote educational opportunities for students in their community. This type of aid is basically free money (no repayment required), and getting a scholarship typically just requires a little research into which ones are available and writing a brief personal essay with your application. Keep in mind that most scholarships do require students to meet academic standards—such as maintaining a certain GPA or full-time enrollment status—to remain eligible to receive funds, but this is not necessarily a bad thing. It can be a source of motivation. One study found that *performance-based scholarships* had positive effects on the student recipients, including increased effort toward studies, reduced financial stress, and an increased confidence in their ability to succeed (Patel & Rudd, 2012). These effects can cause an increase in course enrollment and credits earned over time, helping students to meet their educational goals.

Institutional aid may come in a variety of forms, including scholarships, emergency loans, grants for certain student populations or in times of crisis, or special programs such as free or reduced-cost summer classes or mini sessions. This type of aid will be very specific to the institution, but it is most definitely worth exploring. For instance, colleges affected by natural disasters or public health crises often receive funding from the state or federal government specifically intended to help students in need. In many of these circumstances, you would be surprised how often colleges have trouble giving the money away! Despite publicity and advertisement by the college, it appears many students are simply unaware that this kind of help is out there and practically free for the taking.

Another local option to help pay for college is some type of **work-study program**. In this arrangement, you are essentially a student worker, performing a part-time job or service on your campus. In addition to the wage you will receive, another benefit of this arrangement is that you are on your campus. Spending your work hours on campus means you will have much easier and more frequent access to the services it provides. You are more likely to stay engaged with the library or learning center, your faculty and peers, and your studies. These programs are also guaranteed to provide flexible hours for you to attend your classes, as that is the whole nature of the agreement. Many employers do not quite grasp this concept or simply can't afford to give you the flexibility you need to attend your classes.

A final option of local aid to consider is **state aid**. Once again, this can take many forms and will be unique to your state of residency. Almost every state has at least one grant or scholarship available, and many have a long list of programs to assist their residents (National Association of Student Financial Aid Administrators, n.d.). The National Association of Student Financial Aid Administrators provides a great resource on their website for exploring aid options available in your state: https://www.nasfaa.org/State_Financial_Aid_Programs.

Federal Aid Options

Even though plenty of local aid options exist, many students still need to tap into sources of federal assistance to make ends meet. In fact, federal aid is the most common form of financial assistance utilized by students at U.S. colleges and universities. You should definitely explore your local sources of funding, but there is nothing wrong with utilizing federal funds as well. When it comes to local versus federal aid, the good news is you don't have to choose between one type or the other. In fact, studies indicate that students who receive a combination of federal, state, and institutional aid have the highest rates of success, and this seems to be particularly true for low-income students (Campbell et al., 2017). There are several different types of federal aid available, but the process for applying for all of them begins in the exact same place: the Free Application for Federal Student Aid, more famously known as FAFSA.

The FAFSA is the only way you can apply for all forms of federal student aid, and the schools you list on your FAFSA will use the information you enter to determine your financial need and calculate how much federal funding you are eligible to receive. Chances are, you may have already filled out a FAFSA to acquire federal aid. If so, get used to it, because you will need to fill one out every year you are in enrolled in college to keep receiving the aid you need. The FAFSA becomes available in October for the following school year and it's best to fill it out as soon as possible as some aid may be awarded on a first come, first served basis.

Here are the basic steps for completing your FAFSA and receiving aid:

1. Go to fafsa.gov to complete the online application (*note*: you will need some personal and tax information that you can usually retrieve automatically from the IRS during the process).
2. After you complete and submit your FAFSA, you will receive your Student Aid Report (SAR), which summarizes the information you entered. Review your SAR and make any corrections if needed.
3. At this point, your school will review the FAFSA application to determine the types of federal aid you are eligible to receive.
4. Finally, you will receive an award letter from your institution explaining the different types of federal aid the college is offering you (the offer may also include state and institutional aid).

That's pretty much it! From the award letter, you select the types and amounts of aid you wish to receive and move forward with your education.

Types of Federal Aid

Before we conclude this section, let's take a minute to discuss the two main types of federal aid you may be offered. Knowing the differences and implications of these types can have an enormous impact on your future financial situation for many years to come.

- **Grants** are *free* money awards that do not have to be repaid. These are the absolute ideal type of aid and should be your number one choice from any federal or local source. By far, the most prominent type of federal grant out there is the Pell Grant. In the 2019–2020 school year, nearly one-third (31%) of all U.S. undergraduate students received this type of grant (Duffin, 2021). Pell grants are eligible to undergraduate students who display significant financial need, meaning their expected family contribution for tuition is much lower than their cost of attendance. The amount you receive may also depend on your enrollment status (full time or part time) and whether you plan to attend a full academic year or not.
- **Loans** are *not free* money—they do have to be repaid. With interest. **Interest** is basically the convenience charge that you pay to the lender as the cost for borrowing money. Undergraduate federal loans come in two basic types: subsidized and unsubsidized. Subsidized loans are available for those in greater financial need and are preferred to unsubsidized because they will cost you less in the long run. The interest on subsidized loans is actually paid by the government while you are enrolled in college, whereas unsubsidized loans begin accruing interest immediately and you are responsible for paying that interest. For this reason, it is essential to utilize all subsidized loan money before taking out unsubsidized loans.

Student Loans: The Dangers of Over-Borrowing

Due to the rising costs of higher education, many students are unable to afford college even after utilizing local sources of aid and maxing out their Pell grants. In the United States, nearly 70% of the undergraduate class of 2019 took out some form of student loan and graduated with an average debt of almost $30,000 (Hall, 2021). According to Scholarship America (2021), there are currently some 37 million Americans with student loan debt totaling a staggering 1.7 trillion dollars! By lowering their credit scores and their spending power, this national crisis severely hinders the ability of college graduates to participate in growing the economy. If not managed properly, excessive loans and the interest they accumulate can become financially crippling, greatly affecting a graduate's ability to provide for their family and invest in their future. Unfortunately, the problem is all too common.

Although the situation is not exactly ideal, student loans have become a necessary tool for affording and completing a college degree in many cases. Considering the stats we mentioned earlier regarding the earning potential of college graduates, taking out loans can be worth the risk as long as you take the necessary precautions to protect your financial future. The key thing is to be as careful as possible

Success Tip

Check out this very simple example to illustrate the concept of interest rates on student loans: Let's say you borrow $1,000 and your loan has a 4% interest rate. After graduation, you will owe the lender the $1,000 back plus $40 in interest (4% of $1,000 is $40). This may not sound like too much, but if you borrow tens of thousands of dollars, it really adds up! This is why it's so crucial to carefully consider how much money you borrow and what type of loan you are signing up for. We'll revisit both of these ideas in the next subsection.

from the very beginning of the borrowing process! Here are some basic guidelines to follow that can help prevent you from falling into the trap of long-term, unmanageable loan debt.

Student Loan Borrower's Guidelines

1. **Use free money first.** Exhaust all options for scholarships, grants, or any other type of free financial aid before resorting to student loans.
2. **Choose subsidized loans over unsubsidized.** Remember, subsidized loans will *not* accrue interest while you are in school, saving you thousands of dollars on your final loan bill.
3. **Avoid private loans at all costs.** Private loans (those offered outside of the FAFSA system) can be extremely predatory and will almost always have a higher interest rate than federal loans.
4. **BORROW ONLY WHAT YOU NEED!** Worthy of all caps because it truly is that important. This is one of the most common and critical mistakes that students make in the borrowing process. Remember, the more money you borrow, the more interest will also come along with it, and you will have to pay *all* of it back someday.

Hopefully, you now understand a little more about how to manage your federal student loans *if* it is necessary to go that route. Once you graduate or if you drop below half-time enrollment, you will be required to complete student loan exit counseling through the FAFSA system to be sure you understand your loan repayment obligations. It's also worth noting that the U.S. government offers a Public Service Loan Forgiveness program, which can wipe your student debt clean after 10 years of repayment if you are employed in a public service capacity, including education. Finally, just like we discussed with the admissions process, if you are uncertain or unclear on any issues related to financial aid, the best possible thing you can do is contact your financial aid department. Once again, these individuals are there to serve you, and they are the most qualified and best suited support system available for help at your unique institution.

The Grand Tour: A Bird's Eye View of Your Campus

In this chapter, we have focused primarily on the offices you will encounter upon initial entry into your community college experience. However, there are many other services and departments that work together to maintain a thriving campus environment and each one of them is worthy of a chapter of their own. We will address some of these later in more detail, but for now, let's conclude Chapter 2 by taking a quick bird's eye view of your institution and explore some common areas that exist on most community college campuses.

Activity 2.2 *Virtual Campus Tour*

In this activity, we'll take a broader look at some of the offices and services you're likely to find on campus, with the objective of becoming more familiar with your community college environment. Use

(Continued)

Activity 2.2 (*Continued*)

your institution's webpage and your own personal knowledge to determine as much of the following information as you can. (Of course, you can physically tour the campus as well.)

On a separate sheet of paper, give the answers to as many of the following items as possible related to your campus environment. If the office or service listed does not exist at your college, you can simply put "not applicable" or "does not exist" for the answer. Happy hunting!

1. Give the contact information (phone number and email) for your admissions and advising offices. Where are they located on your campus? Give the contact info for their directors.
2. Give the contact information (phone number and email) for your financial aid office. Where is it located on your campus? Give the contact info for its director.
3. Give the hours and phone number for your campus library. What types of materials can you check out there?
4. If you have a learning or tutoring center, give the hours and describe the services it provides.
5. For your current major, give the name and contact information for your program director, department chair, or dean.
6. How many academic programs do you have on campus? Give the names of all academic program directors, department chairs, and deans, and specify which programs they oversee.
7. How many technical programs do you have on campus? Give the names of all academic program directors, department chairs, and deans and specify which programs they oversee.
8. What is the name of your student center? Give the name and contact information for its director. List all student organizations on campus. Indicate any you may be interested in joining.
9. If your campus has a cafeteria or food service of any kind, what is it called and what types of food products do they offer? If you've been there, what are some of your favorite menu items?
10. Give the hours of your campus gym or fitness center. What types of services/equipment do they offer and what are some of your favorites?
11. Give the contact information for campus security.
12. Give the name and contact information for your college president.

End-of-Chapter Questions

1. **Recall.** Name four types of local financial aid and list several possible benefits of performance-based scholarships. What is the fundamental difference between grants and loans? Briefly describe the difference between subsidized and unsubsidized loans; which type is more favorable and why?

2. **Engage.** Connect with another classmate and discuss how you went about choosing your current academic or technical major. Did someone or something influence you to choose this path? Have an informal conversation on why you chose this and what you hope to

gain from it. If you're not quite sure yet, discuss your interests and possible majors/future career choices. Document your classmate's responses in four to six sentences.

3. **Reflect.** Describe what you learned from the Activity 2.2. Did you explore your campus physically or on the web? In a 100-word response, reflect on any new facts you learned about your college and discuss any features or services you would like to take advantage of and why.

4. **Create.** Put yourself in the shoes of an academic advisor. Now create a list of at least five questions you would ask a new student in order to help them choose their path (and their classes). These can be personal or technical questions. There are no wrong answers here but provide a brief justification (one or two sentences) for each one describing why you think it would be effective.

References

Campbell, C., Cochrane, D., Love, I., & Bruecker, E. (2017). *Aiding success: The role of federal and state financial aid in supporting California community college students.* Association of Community College Trustees. https://www.acct.org/files/Publications/2017/ACCT_TICAS_CCCCO_Aiding_Students_2017.pdf

Duffin, E. (2021, November 2). *Share of federal Pell Grant recipients U.S. 2010-2021.* Statista.com. https://www.statista.com/statistics/235409/recipients-of-federal-pell-grants-in-the-us/

Hall, I. (2021, June 24). *Risk of over-borrowing on student loans.* Sholarships.com. https://www.scholarships.com/news/risks-of-over-borrowing-on-student-loans

National Association of Student Financial Aid Administrators. (n.d.). *State financial aid programs.* https://www.nasfaa.org/State_Financial_Aid_Programs

National Center for Education Statistics. (2022, May). *Annual earnings by educational attainment.* https://nces.ed.gov/programs/coe/indicator/cba/annual-earnings

OneClass. (2020, June 1). Ability to afford school? [Blog post] https://oneclass.com/blog/featured/179420-how-has-the-pandemic-affected-your-ability-to-afford-school3F.en.html

Patel, R., & Rudd, T. (2012, November). *Can scholarships alone help students succeed? Lessons from two New York City community colleges.* MDRC. https://www.mdrc.org/publication/can-scholarships-alone-help-students-succeed

Scholarship America. (2021, January). *The far-reaching impact of the student debt crisis.* https://scholarshipamerica.org/blog/the-far-reaching-impact-of-the-student-debt-crisis/

Thomas, C. (2017, February 22). *Academic advising and institutional success.* Academic Advising Today. https://nacada.ksu.edu/Resources/Academic-Advising-Today/View-Articles/Academic-Advising-and-Institutional-Success.aspx

U.S. Department of Education. (2017, February 10). *Community college facts at a glance.* https://www2.ed.gov/about/offices/list/ovae/pi/cclo/ccfacts.html

Young-Jones, A. D., Burt, T. D., Dixon, S., & Hawthorne, M. J. (2013). Academic advising: Does it really impact student success? *Quality Assurance in Education, 21*(1), 7–19. https://doi.org/10.1108/09684881311293034

Image Credits

IMG 2.1: Copyright © 2016 Depositphotos/monkeybusiness.

CHAPTER 3

Time to Shine

Setting Priorities, Making Good Choices, and Managing Your Time Effectively

Image 3.1

Introduction

In Chapter 3, we take a deep dive into how we utilize one of the most precious resources you have in this life: your time. How you prioritize activities and spend your time can literally make or break your community college experience. It can mean the difference between happiness and success or failure and stress. Let's choose the former path and take a closer look at how we choose to spend the time we have with the goal of finding areas for improvement to ensure the success of your journey. This chapter will provide real life testimony, practical strategies, and opportunities for personal reflection and growth around the following themes:

- Analyzing priorities in your daily routine
- Making good choices to affect positive results
- Managing your time to optimize academic and personal success, in general

Here's a brief summary of the main sections you'll encounter in Chapter 3: In "Hard Lessons," Dr. K (the author) recounts his own lack of time management skills as a beginning college student and describes how improving these skills resulted in positive change on multiple levels. "A Day in the Life" asks the student to consider their daily life choices and the various responsibilities they manage, and includes Activity 3.1—Mapping Your Daily Routine, Activity 3.2—Analyzing Your Routine, and Activity 3.3—Reflecting on Your Routine. "Time Management 101: 5 Key Practices" provides a list of proven, effective time management strategies for the student's consideration. And, finally, in "A Day in the Life—Revisited," the student is asked to take all information and their reflections from the chapter to design an improved daily routine template for their own experimentation and personal benefit. Enjoy!

And you run, and you run to catch up with the sun, but it's sinking.
Racing around to come up behind you again.

—Pink Floyd, "Time"

So there I was, sitting at home studying on a warm spring night about 20 years ago from the time of this publication. It was the second semester of my freshman year in college; I was 19 years old. This was a typical Wednesday evening, unremarkable for the most part except for one significant detail: my first trigonometry exam of the semester was going down the next morning and I was, let's just say, not ready. My attendance in the course was spotty, I wasn't really keeping up with my assignments, and I hadn't mastered the material in any sense. But hey, at least I was making an effort to cram it all in the night before, right?

Despite being a bit behind, I figured if I spent enough time working through the homework I should have already completed, I just might be able to pull off a decent grade. Maybe not an A but I felt a B was within striking distance—I could pull it off! And you know what, I might have. There was at least a glimmer of hope. That is, until ... the phone rang.

It was one of my best buddies on the other end. This was a guy I had known since grade school and ran with all throughout junior high and high school. Not too long before this night, we had walked across the stage together at our high school graduation; years later, he would be the best man at my wedding.

(Continued)

(Continued)

Anyway, as it turned out—would you believe it?—they were having people over at his house that night. Well, technically, in the barn behind the house—a situation not terribly unusual in Southeast Texas.

This particular barn at my friend's place, however, was unusually cool. It was stocked full of his dad's vintage surfboards hanging neatly suspended from aging rafters; there was an old record player, and posters of blues legends like Stevie Ray Vaughan and Muddy Waters were tacked to the walls; we had set up a TV with a gaming system hooked up and ready to go. And we had instruments. In this space, we could listen to music, strum guitars, play video games, and generally indulge in all the newfound privileges of our post-high school freedom, which included hanging out late on a weeknight. There was no special occasion, but several of my good friends were going to be there, and I was starting to feel an acute case of FOMO ("fear of missing out") coming on pretty strong ...

Hard Lessons

Greetings, folks! Dr. K, here. What you just read was a little snippet from my own time management struggles early on in my college experience. You may be wondering which path I chose that night. Did I do the right thing? Did I prioritize the situation and act accordingly? Did I make the painfully obvious and correct decision to stay home and study at 9:00 p.m. on a Wednesday night before my first trig exam, or did I drive across town for no good reason to hang out with friends who I saw literally all the time?

You probably already know the answer, but to make a long story short, I ended up sitting right back in that same trigonometry class the next semester. (SPOILER ALERT: It was *not* because I enjoyed it so much that I just had to have another taste. I made a D in the course and, believe me, I earned it.)

Of course, I didn't end up in that situation solely because of my poor choice on that random Wednesday night, but it was decisions like this one, along with my general lack of structured priorities, that taught me some tough but very important truths about college, and life in general. Looking back (although I still shake my head a little), I am thankful that at least I *did* learn from hard lessons like this one before it was too late.

Seeing the Light

After fumbling around for a while and beating my head against the same walls, I gradually discovered that my academic life became much easier when I made a few simple but definitive adjustments in my general routine and how I approached my classes. And not only did things get easier, when I set new priorities and learned how to better manage my time, the stress I felt toward my entire situation at college decreased tenfold! This alone made it worthwhile. When I started making better choices and sticking to my new system, increased academic self-confidence and much better grades flowed as a natural consequence of my actions. Perhaps even better still, I came to truly enjoy and appreciate my college experience, which had a direct impact on my overall quality of life. None of this would come as a shock to higher education researchers, who began describing the positive effects of time management skills on college achievement, stress levels, and life satisfaction at least several decades ago (Britton & Tesser, 1991; Macan et al., 1990).

Good News

The little setback described above was my failure, and I had to own it. Eventually, I did successfully pass trigonometry and many other difficult courses beyond it. And although I learned some impactful formative lessons early on in my college career, the mistakes I made still proved very costly in terms of two extremely valuable resources: *time* and *money*.

The good news I want to share is that you don't have to learn the hard way. In fact, I don't recommend it at all. By setting priorities and holding yourself accountable, you can skip right over the rocky start I put myself through. In this way, you'll get more out of your academic journey *and* you'll get further down the road to completion or transfer in a shorter amount of time. It's literally a win-win. Later in the chapter, we'll discuss the actual changes and practices I put in place to improve my situation as well as additional proven strategies for effectively managing your time.

I hope you enjoyed this somewhat colorful account of my early college experience and the lessons I learned (eventually). But that's enough about me for now—let's talk about you. After all, this is about *your* journey and *your* experience. Knowing, firsthand, how much potential is out there if you work hard and make the right decisions, I am beyond excited for you.

A Day in the Life

What does a typical day look like—and feel like—for you? Do you consider yourself productive and/or high energy, just checking off boxes and straight up getting things done? Are you often tired or constantly "behind the eight ball," barely able to keep up with deadlines and responsibilities? More importantly, are you happy?

Many of our days may flow in between the two extremes just described—sometimes in a single day! And this dynamic changes as we move through the seasons of our lives, in and out of educational institutions, jobs, personal phases, and domestic situations. Regardless of where you're at, now is a good time to take a very close and brutally honest look at your daily routine in hopes of finding opportunities for improvement, big or small.

A lot of us can probably relate to the Pink Floyd lyric at the start of the chapter—running as hard as we can just to get through the rigors of a normal day, only to go to bed, wake up, and do it all over again. We often say things like "I just don't have time to get to that" or "there aren't enough hours in a day." While this may hold some truth, it is also true that we all have the same amount of time in a given day.

Of course, many of us do have real life obligations that legitimately hinder our ability to study or be productive during large chunks of our daily time. We know that, due to these various responsibilities, most community college students attend part time, and evidence suggests that time management strategies are particularly important for this group (Lane & Lane, 2001). We also know that community college students are slightly older, the average age being 29, compared to the majority of university students who are under 25 (Vlasova, 2022). According to a recent survey, most students who are also parents attend a community college over university, and more than one-fourth (26%) of all two-year college students have dependent children at home (Ashford, 2020). A report from the Institute for Women's Policy Research (2013) revealed that over 40% of student-parents also work full time, and over half of them spend some 30 hours per week on childcare-related activities. Interestingly, this same report revealed that student-parents and those who are older than average tend to have higher GPAs than their younger, nonparent counterparts.

Undoubtedly, many of you out there are juggling a lot of responsibilities outside of the classroom. Trust me, we can relate. Both authors of this book had full-time academic jobs and families while completing our graduate studies, and both of us had multiple children at home. My youngest daughter was born right in the middle of my doctoral program! Getting an education is definitely not easy—it requires a lot of hard work and sacrifice. But it is 100% worth it in the end, especially if you're doing something you truly believe in to better yourself, your family, and the people around you. The benefits of a higher education are real—for you and your present or future family. In fact, research indicates that increasing your educational attainment leads to higher pay, greater access to employment opportunities, and an increased likelihood that your child will also pursue a college degree (Attewell et al., 2009).

The Power of Choices

Whether you have a lot of time to devote to your studies or relatively little, it's important to analyze your daily routine and look for ways to improve. In fact, if you're strapped for time, I'd suggest it may be *more* important to look closely at your schedule and locate areas where even minor adjustments can be made to enhance productivity. Retired NASA physicist and consciousness researcher Thomas Campbell spoke of "tiny positive or negative increments in the quality of [our] intent, over many thousands of choices" that add up over time to either increase or decrease your overall effectiveness and quality of life (Campbell, 2003). This means that small decisions matter, and grabbing even 15, 20, or 30 minutes throughout the day to focus on academic priorities can have a huge impact, especially if these mini sessions are planned out and observed consistently.

Life is all about choices and this certainly applies to your academic life at the community or state college. On some level, it really is quite simple: good choices lead to positive outcomes; bad choices lead to negative results and more stress. We all know this, intuitively, and most of the time, if you really pay attention, you can *feel* whether the choice you are making is a good one or not. Should I read this chapter before the quiz tomorrow or spend the next hour on TikTok? Should I work through these algebra problems I don't quite understand or go on a four-hour Netflix binge? You get the picture. So, let's have some fun, shall we? In Activity 3.1, below, we're going to dive into our routine for a typical day and try to identify spots where we could make better decisions and improve our chances for success. It's important to be honest here—this is a judgment-free zone—and if you find you have a lot of room for improvement, good! That's the point of this exercise. Challenge yourself and think of this like a game and it

Activity 3.1 *Mapping Your Daily Routine*

Okay, gang, time to play. Let's establish two things, up front, heading into this exercise: one, we're not going to judge each other based on our routines (we can all find ways to improve), and two, it's important to be honest—this activity will not be nearly as effective otherwise. Everyone here is on their own journey and, hence, none of our schedules will look exactly alike. I've been doing this assignment for years in my course and I'm always amazed by the vast differences I see in the daily lives of my students—a true testament to the diversity of your demographic! The truly inspiring part for me is seeing that just about everyone learns something about themselves and identifies areas for improvement through deeper reflection.

So here are the rules. In Table 3.1, below, map out a typical day in the life, from the time you wake up until you go to bed at night (or, in some cases, maybe in the morning). Choose an actual day in recent memory that is consistent with your normal routine and account for what you did in every waking hour on the table provided below. If possible, provide a brief description of what each activity entails in the third column ("Description") to help paint the picture. Finally, in the last column ("Category"), define what type of activity is occurring in each hour of your day. After completing the table, we will add up the total time for each category of our activities, then reflect on what we are seeing and how we could make improvements to enhance productivity and quality in our daily lives.

Choose from the following categories for defining your activities in the last column on the table:

1. **It's a *must.*** These are things you simply have to do in the course of your daily routine. Category 1 would include things like cooking and eating, basic hygiene (shower, dental care, etc.), going to work, any childcare-related activities, or any other activity deemed essential in your day. (Note: we will address sleep later on in the reflection.)
2. **I *really* need to.** This includes other activities that, although extremely important, are slightly less obligatory than items in Category 1. For Category 2, consider things like studying or attending class (technically, these are optional), doing house- or yardwork, spending time with friends or loved ones, playing with your kids, walking the dog, et cetera.
3. **I'd *really* like to.** As you can probably see, we are getting further down the list of priorities and into the more leisurely end of the spectrum. Category 3 might contain items such as exercise or outdoor activities, self-care (beauty treatments, massage, meditation, etc.), reading a novel or work of nonfiction (not course related), watching a documentary, any artistic endeavor (such as drawing, painting, writing, or playing an instrument), or just spending time in nature (one of my favorites).
4. **I *probably* shouldn't.** These are activities that we may enjoy a great deal but are generally unproductive and not truly beneficial. For most of us, Category 4 will probably involve some form (or forms) of passive media, such as social media, watching or streaming shows or movies of no real educational value, playing video games, randomly searching the internet, or going down a YouTube rabbit hole, among others. Other Category 4 activities might include hanging out at places we probably don't really need to be, from a productivity standpoint (the mall, movie theater, pool hall, bar or club, bowling alley, Starbucks, etc.).

(Continued)

Activity 3.1 *(Continued)*

Table 3.1

List your activities for each waking hour of a typical day and do your best to briefly describe and categorize them. There are 20 rows provided—hopefully enough for you to list the hours and your activities from the time you wake until you go to bed. Feel free to adjust the table, if needed. Add a brief description and category for each activity but don't sweat the details—this exercise is for you. It's totally fine to have more than one activity in a given hour; just try to specify how many minutes are involved so we can add them up for each category later in our analysis.

Hour	Activity	Description	Category (1–4)

(Continued)

Activity 3.1 *(Continued)*

Table 3.1 *(CONTINUED)*

Hour	Activity	Description	Category (1–4)

Activity 3.2 *Analyzing Your Routine*

All done? Nice—now the real work can begin. On a separate sheet of paper (or on your electronic device), add up all the hours and minutes for each of the four categories. What do you see? In which categories do you invest the most time and does this seem reasonable and effective to you? Is it easy to spot some areas where you can be more productive or is it difficult to find the time to improve your routine? Before you write up your reflection on this activity, read over and consider the following practical tips on the four categories we used to define our daily actions:

Category 1 Considerations (It's a *must*)

Many of these items truly are "a must," and we simply can't get by without doing them. I am often floored by some of my students (usually the slightly older ones with children) who seem to have nearly an entire day full of Category 1 activities.

You may not be able to reduce these much, or even at all, but there are still at least a couple things to consider here:

- Are all of these items truly essential all the time?
- If they are, could you possibly reduce the time you spend doing them in some way?

(Continued)

Activity 3.2 (*Continued*)

Again, it is understood that some of these items will be nonnegotiable. For example, children are absolutely essential parts of our lives and deserve all the care and attention we can provide. However, there are occasions where you may need to seek out special assistance or support, especially if you have an upcoming exam, research paper, or project due. If you don't have family or friends to lean on and a daycare or sitter is not feasible, you may look to the community college itself. Nearly half (47%) of two-year colleges reportedly house on-site childcare centers (Institute for Women's Policy Research, 2013), and many others offer financial assistance for student-parents in need. This type of college support service could also provide you the opportunity to attend class in person, which may be more beneficial depending on the nature of the course and your individual learning style.

The other major Category 1 demand on our time is often work-related activity. Providing financial security for yourself and your family is something that many of us simply cannot compromise. However, for individuals who may not need to work a high-intensity, full-time job, or to pick up that extra shift, you may consider if the work you are doing is worth the short-term financial gain if it is jeopardizing your success in the long run—your college completion and a rewarding career beyond. This can be a tough call because practically all of us could use the money at this stage in life! Just be sure that you're not throwing away a shot at the job you really want for the one you currently have. You may have to temporarily accept a little less money with a job that can work around your schedule in order to attain your ultimate goal.

Category 2 Considerations (I *really* need to)

This is a big one, for our purposes, because it includes studying and attending class (or logging in to online courses). Clearly, if you are enrolled in college and committed to your future, you simply have to find the time to address these items. As we mentioned earlier, look for even small windows of opportunity. Do you wait in line at school or soccer practice to pick up your kids, or ever spend the weekend at a baseball tournament with hours of slack time? Have a medical appointment or something else that involves waiting in a lobby? Are you going on a road trip or vacation where your spouse or friend is doing much of the driving? If you answered "yes" to any of these, bring a book! Bring your notes, or just utilize the incredible capacity of your smartphone to access and review course materials. And if you don't have formal, course-related electronic materials provided on a topic, don't be afraid to google it. Of course, you need to be careful of the information sources you choose (see Chapter 7), but the internet is an incredibly powerful tool when used correctly.

If you keep your coursework on your radar and on your mind—even for short increments of time—it *will* pay off. The repetition and engagement will help you to memorize and grasp the material and you will be rewarded for your good choices. If you can regularly schedule study sessions, even short ones, during your day, you will truly begin to see the benefits and the power of this technique. Obviously, as quiz or exam time approaches, you need to dedicate even more time to this category. Certainly, the dishes and laundry have to get done and eventually that yard has to get mowed. But if you look closely, you can likely find more time to devote to your academic success, particularly if this is a troublesome area for you.

(*Continued*)

Activity 3.2 (*Continued*)

Maximizing your time in this category (class attendance and studying in particular) is probably the most important part of this entire activity.

Category 3 Considerations (I'd *really* like to)

Don't sleep on Category 3. This area can be tricky and may be the most complex of the four categories to manage. In no way should you avoid doing these kinds of things altogether; we're just looking for areas in which maybe you are spending a little too much time during a typical weekday. Or, possibly, not enough.

Recall that Category 3 generally contains items that are beneficial to your health and well-being. Although they may not be directly tied to your academic studies, it's safe to say that we all need some level of these self-care activities in our routines to keep us sane, happy, and productive. For example, even just 15–30 minutes of exercise (perhaps followed by 5–10 minutes of breathing and meditation), especially in the morning, can get your mind, body, and motivation where you need them to be. You start the day feeling accomplished, already, and it will give you energy once you get used to a routine.

If exercise is just not your thing or not physically possible, any activity that is creative or therapeutic for you is of great value—even in small doses. Whether it's drawing, reading, knitting, or getting a facial, these activities can "fill our cup" and keep us grounded, happy, and appreciative of our life in the present moment. Like exercise, these things can give us some calmness and clarity and actually enhance productivity once we do get back to work. It's good to recharge the batteries and it's good to actually enjoy your life during the week, even if you are working and going to school. If you choose to view the week as an unpleasant chore that you just have to trudge through in order to get to the weekend, you are missing out on many, many potential days of happiness. And we only get a limited supply of those.

Obviously, during times of intense demand from Category 1 or 2 activities, Category 3 may take a hit and need to be suspended temporarily. But, in general, I would recommend 30 minutes to an hour most weekdays to take care of yourself, if possible. Even if it means waking up a little earlier sometimes.

Category 4 Considerations (I *probably* shouldn't)

You might call this one the "treat yourself" category. Again, we're not saying you should *never* do any of these things—we all indulge on occasion. In fact, some weekend nights spent watching ridiculous movies with the kids or a Netflix series with your spouse or friends, while eating nothing of nutritional value, can be absolutely amazing. It's also pretty safe to assume that the vast majority of us probably spend too much time scrolling social media on occasion (more on this later). All these things are okay ... sort of. Just keep in mind that Category 4 activities have their time and place, and during the week, when you're trying to stay productive and get the truly important tasks done, is probably not the best time to indulge. At the very least, these activities should be minimized as much as possible because, in short, they generally do not get you any closer to your goals and dreams. If you want to achieve great things for yourself and others, staying disciplined and focused is just part of the deal—it is a necessary corequisite.

Activity 3.3 *Reflecting on Your Routine*

Now that you have sketched out your daily routine, analyzed how you spend your time, and read through the practical considerations for the four categories of daily activities, it is time to reflect. Write out your general reaction to how you spend your time. What insights did you have through your analysis of each category? What areas stood out the most to you and, most importantly, where do you see areas for improvement? Be sure to suggest actual adjustments you could make to improve your routine (we will apply these later at the end of the chapter). One more thing to address that was not on Table 3.1: sleep. In your reflection, also make a quick assessment of how much sleep you are typically getting and indicate whether you feel this amount is adequate or not. A 250-word response is suggested, but that's between you and your instructor. Even if you do not consider yourself a great writer, articulating and expressing your thoughts on paper is a very beneficial and insightful exercise.

actually can be kind of fun. The difference here is that the rewards of "winning" this game are real and can have a lasting impact on your future.

Time Management 101: 5 Key Practices

Proper time management is undoubtedly key to a successful college experience, and studies indicate that this is a skill that can be learned and improved upon (Nadinloyi, 2013). Before we wind down, it's time to share with you all a short list of fundamental concepts related to the topic. These are essentially best practices for time management, backed by research literature and reflected in our own experiences. We hope you will consider these practices and add them to your tool kit if you're not using them already. Here they are, in no particular order:

1. **Go to Class.** Seems like a no-brainer, but you'd be surprised how many students fall into the trap of gradually slipping in their attendance until it's too late to climb back up the hill. I was one of these students. This was possibly the single most impactful practice that completely altered the trajectory of my academic journey. When I (Dr. K) decided I was going to force myself to attend every single class meeting I possibly could, everything changed. I made invaluable connections with my instructors and, more importantly, my peers. My GPA soared, and my stress levels tanked—a complete reversal of where these two things were heading prior to this adjustment. Looking at it strictly from a time management perspective, you know you have to invest a certain amount of time to engage with and review the material in every course to be successful. So why not take advantage and do this in the designated meeting time when your instructor is also present? To suggest that classroom attendance may be the most critical factor for academic achievement is not hyperbole. Research has shown that attendance can predict college grades more accurately than other known factors, including high school GPA, SAT scores, study skills, and even the amount of time you spend studying (Credé & Kuncel, 2008; Hezlett et al., 2001). Similarly, in online courses—even when

there are no formal meetings—there is evidence that spending time online engaging with the material is key to success (Ryabov, 2012). The bottom line? Go to class.

2. **Study Early and Often.** Here's another trick I (Dr. K) learned that dramatically improved my test scores and reduced my stress. Another way of saying this is "don't cram." Or, at least, don't rely on cramming alone for success—it will not end well most of the time. Experts suggest that for every hour you spend in class, you should spend at least two hours on your own time studying and preparing for the next meeting. This means for an average three-hour course, you should be studying an additional 4.5 hours per week outside of the classroom. If you can accomplish this, there should be no need to have to cram too much the night before the exam. However, I do recommend kicking it up a notch approximately 1 week before a major exam to ensure your success. In this way, you will be in the driver's seat, and an intense study session a night or two before the test will be more of a review to solidify the information. This position is much more favorable (for your mental health and your grade) compared to pulling a last-minute all-nighter out of desperation and necessity. Football fans should already know that the ol' Hail Mary doesn't work very often.

3. **Procrastination is the Enemy.** It's no secret that doing nothing is infinitely easier than doing something. In the short term, at least. Shrugging off or delaying responsibilities may feel a little dangerous or exciting in the moment, or maybe we tell ourselves little white lies about how we "definitely have time to do that later," despite not knowing what the immediate future may hold. The truth is we have no idea what we may be faced with unexpectedly, and if you have the time to complete a task, it is *always* better to just take care of it right then and there, so you don't pay for it later. Once again, this is better for productivity and performance as well as peace of mind. Procrastination is definitely not your friend in the college setting, and this will continue to be true throughout your adult life. Related to the previous practice, research confirms that students who procrastinate on their studies, rather than spacing out study times more evenly, perform much more poorly on quizzes and exams (Ariely & Wertenbroch, 2002). But this is about more than just study habits. Avoiding procrastination applies equally to *any* task related to your college experience, whether it's applying for financial aid, registering for classes, purchasing your textbooks, asking your professor about a concept you don't understand—the list goes on. In short, if you avoid procrastination and take care of things as soon as possible, you'll avoid creating unnecessary problems for yourself *and* you'll free up more time to accomplish things later on.

4. **Use a Planner.** In fact, use several. With all the numerous responsibilities you now have to keep up with—in your academic and personal life—it

Success Tip

Around my sophomore year, I (Dr. K) discovered the power of a physical planning notebook (low cost and available almost everywhere) to keep track of important dates and have not looked back since. Personally, I prefer the type that displays one week at a time to give a nice overview of important tasks in manageable chunks. I also use a monthly desktop calendar for an expanded view of what's coming down the pipe.

pays to have multiple systems in place to keep it all straight. Students who actually plan and keep track of their time with organizational tools tend to study more efficiently, stay on top of their tasks, and score higher on exams (Van den Hurk, 2006). There is almost certainly a calendar feature in your campus email system (Outlook, Google Mail, etc.)—use it. This is a great place to enter appointments, study sessions, due dates, and reminders of all kinds, *and* has the added benefit of getting you into your campus email account, regularly, where critical messages may be waiting. Download the app for this account on your smartphone and you'll have the ability to check in and keep up with your schedule virtually anytime, anywhere. I simply could not function without this incredibly valuable tool.

5. **Watch the Social Media.** Yes, we touched on this earlier in Category 4 Considerations, but the power and influence of social media is now so ubiquitous (and often problematic) that it warrants a second look. Nearly half (48%) of adults ages 18–29 indicated in a recent survey that they were "almost constantly" online (Perrin & Atske, 2021), and this figure is up about 10% from the same survey just two years prior. Studies indicate that social networks can take up the majority of free time for college students (Talaue et al., 2018), and excessive use of social media is generally shown to negatively affect academic results (Habes et al., 2018). It's pretty shocking when students reveal spending several hours at a time on social media sites, usually in the morning or at the end of their day. That being said, the honesty is appreciated, and we realize this is not unusual for young people today—it is simply part of the culture. As indicated previously, we are not suggesting you refrain from these activities altogether. Social media can be a valuable tool for learning and education on certain topics, as well as a medium for valuable networking and self-expression. They key thing is to pay attention. If you catch yourself scrolling aimlessly for hours on end, or if you notice you are relying on these platforms for validating your self-worth or opinions, it's probably a good time to step back, take a break, and try to reduce the amount of time you are spending, for your own sake. The truth is social media is not going anywhere, and the younger generation (millennials and up) will have to learn to self-regulate this phenomenon more carefully than any of their predecessors.

A Day in the Life—Revisited

We've covered quite a bit of ground in this chapter, and we hope you've had the chance to reflect and build upon your ability to prioritize activities, make better choices, and maximize your time for success. In this final section, it's time to apply everything you've learned in the chapter (from the information provided and your own reflections) to create an improved daily routine template. Take the basic design of Table 3.1 and map out a new game plan for how you would like to spend most weekdays more effectively. Incorporate the improvements you discussed and Activity 3.1 Reflection, making as many of these adjustments to your schedule as you can. Keep it reasonable, but try your best to generate improvement and productivity in your academic and personal routine. After you draft this new schedule, the rest is on you. Try it out! There is certainly no harm in at least giving it a shot. Challenge yourself and consider it a personal experiment to try to do a little better. Don't be afraid to make minor adjustments as needed. Give your new and improved routine an honest effort for a week or two and you may be surprised by the results. We sincerely hope that you are.

End-of-Chapter Questions

1. **Recall.** According to research, which of the 5 Key Practices listed in the chapter most likely has the greatest impact on academic success? Based on information in the chapter, describe (in your own words) why it is important to avoid procrastination and list several areas in which this might apply to your academic life.
2. **Engage.** Swap your improved daily routine template with another student in the class. Discuss with each other what you learned through initial analysis and reflection, then document any feedback or response received from the other person.
3. **Reflect.** Overall, which concept or concepts stood out most to you in the chapter? In which area do you envision yourself needing improvement and, conversely, what do you feel you are already doing well? Describe in your own words.
4. **Create.** Picture yourself 5–10 years down the road in the desired career and lifestyle you would like to pursue. Describe or map out your ideal daily routine at this stage in your life. Don't be afraid to dream big—you have the ability to create the future you want for yourself.

References

Ariely, D., & Wertenbroch, K. (2002). Procrastination, deadlines, and performance: Self-control by precommitment. *Psychological Science, 13*(3), 219–224. https://doi.org/10.1111/1467-9280.00441

Ashford, E. (2020, May 13). *Student parents underserved.* Community College Daily. https://www.ccdaily.com/2020/05/student-parents-underserved/

Attewell, P., Lavin, D., Domina, T., & Levey, T. (2009). *Passing the torch: Does higher education for the disadvantaged pay off across the generations?* Russell Sage Foundation.

Britton, B. K., & Tesser, A. (1991). Effects of time-management practices on college grades. *Journal of Educational Psychology, 83*(3), 405–410. https://doi.org/10.1037/0022-0663.83.3.405

Campbell, T. (2003). *My big theory of everything: Awakening.* Lightning Strike Books.

Crede, M., & Kuncel, N. R. (2008). Study habits, skills, and attitudes: The third pillar supporting collegiate academic performance. *Perspectives on Psychological Science, 3*(6), 425–453. https://doi.org/10.1111/j.1745-6924.2008.00089.x

Habes, M., Alghizzawi, M., Khalaf, R., Salloum, S., & Ghani, M. A. (2018). The relationship between social media and academic performance: Facebook perspective. *International Journal of Information Technology and Language Studies, 2*(1), 12–18. http://journals.sfu.ca/ijitls

Hezlett, S. A., Kuncel, N. R., Vey, M. A., Ahart, A., Ones, D. S., & Campbell, J. P. (2001, April). The predictive validity of the SAT: A comprehensive meta-analysis. In D. S. Ones & S. A. Hezlett (Chairs), *Predicting performance: The interface of I/O psychology and educational research.*

Symposium conducted at the annual conference of the Society for Industrial and Organizational Psychology, San Diego, CA.

Institute for Women's Policy Research. (2013, March). *College students with children are common and face many challenges in completing higher education.* https://files.eric.ed.gov/fulltext/ED556715.pdf

Lane, J., & Lane, L. (2001). Self-efficacy and academic performance. *Social Behavior and Personality, 29*(7), 687–694. https://doi.org/10.2224/sbp.2001.29.7.687

Macan, T. H., Shahani, C., Dipboye, R. L., & Phillips, A. P. (1990). College students' time management: Correlations with academic performance and stress. *Journal of Educational Psychology, 82*(4), 760–768. https://doi.org/10.1037/0022-0663.82.4.760

Nadinloyi, K. B., Hajloo, N., Garamaleki, N. S., & Sadeghi, H. (2013). The study efficacy of time management training on increase academic time management of students. *Procedia Social and Behavioral Sciences, 84*(2013), 134–138.

Perrin, A., & Atske, S. (2021, March 26). *About three-in-ten U.S. adults say they are "almost constantly" online.* Pew Research Center. https://www.pewresearch.org/fact-tank/2021/03/26/about-three-in-ten-u-s-adults-say-they-are-almost-constantly-online/

Ryabov, I. (2012). The effect of time online on grades in online sociology courses. *Journal of Online Learning and Teaching, 8*(1), 13–23.

Talaue, G. M., AlSaad, A., AlRushaidan, N., AlHugail, A., & AlFahhad, S. (2018). The impact of social media on academic performance of selected college students. *International Journal of Advanced Information Technology, 8*(4), 27–35. https://doi.org/10.5121/ijait.2018.8503

Van den Hurk, M. (2006). The relation between self-regulated strategies and individual study time, prepared participation and achievement in a problem-based curriculum. *Active Learning in Higher Education, 7*(2), 155–169. https://doi.org/10.1177/1469787406064752

Vlasova, H. (2022, June 23). *Community college statistics – 2022.* Admissionly.com. https://admissionly.com/community-college-statistics/

Image Credits

IMG 3.1: Copyright © 2016 Depositphotos/Rawpixel.

CHAPTER 4

Making Connections

Why Engagement and Communication Will Be Key to Your Academic Success

Image 4.1

Introduction

One of the most rewarding of aspects of community college, and in life, is forging meaningful connections through communication with others. Connecting with others in your campus environment can bring about both personal satisfaction and academic advantage. In order to optimize these benefits, it's important to have tolerance and understanding toward others and to learn the general types of interactions you should expect to encounter and the basic rules of engagement that govern them. Along these lines, Chapter 4 will revolve around the following themes:

- Understanding the importance of cultural diversity on your campus and the value of treating others with respect
- Interacting with your peers and the many advantages of these connections
- Interacting with instructors respectfully for the mutual benefit of both parties

Here's a brief summary of the main sections contained in Chapter 4: In "Cultural Understanding and the Golden Rule," importance of acting with understanding and respect toward others at the community college is discussed. "Engaging With Peers" describes the various types of student interactions to anticipate on campus, along with the benefits of each, and includes Activity 4.1—Student Interaction Reflection. Finally, "Communicating With Instructors" presents the idea of the student-instructor balance in general classroom commitments and gives students guidelines for how to most effectively communicate with their instructor. This section also contains Activity 4.2—The Perfect Instructor Email, which provides students a hands-on opportunity to apply the instructor email communication guidelines covered in the section.

In a real sense all life is inter-related. We are all caught in an inescapable network of mutuality, tied in a single garment of destiny.

—Dr. Martin Luther King Jr.

Cultural Understanding and the Golden Rule

We live in a world that is more culturally diverse than ever before and it's only growing more so by the day, with over half of all K–12 students now being children of color (National Center for Education Statistics, 2022b). America is truly a melting pot. Nearly every race and ethnicity migrated here from somewhere else and the lines of distinction between us tend to blur as we mix our genetics, customs, and social practices. We should be proud and celebrate our diversity as a nation as this is one of our great strengths that led to the prominence we enjoy in the world today—economically, culturally, and educationally.

As we mentioned in Chapter 1, the community college is also an institution of great diversity, containing roughly the same representation of different races and gender ratios we currently see in our country as a whole, with the demographic trends also moving toward greater diversity. This means that no matter which culture or high school you came from, you are likely to encounter a greater variety of students (and instructors) with ethnic and cultural backgrounds unlike your own. This is an exciting prospect and a perfect opportunity for personal growth that can shape you and complement the academic and intellectual growth you are also destined to experience on this journey.

Although not for the first time, our society is experiencing a time of great change that includes some degree of civil unrest, tension, and even division as deep-seated issues have emerged onto the surface of our societal consciousness. It is for these reasons that there exists a need for patience, openness, and tolerance to bring about healing and a greater understanding of one another. As Dr. King famously stated, we truly are all "inter-related" and interconnected. In this same quote, he expanded upon this idea stating that "whatever affects one directly, affects all indirectly." This implies that our actions and opinions toward others can spread all the way around our human community and eventually come right back to us.

For these reasons, it's important to approach your campus community members with the best of intentions. Make it a point to reach out and try to connect with others from different backgrounds. Listen to their stories and try to learn from them. Share yours with them as well. Try to accept the fact that from your own personal perspective, you can never know exactly what their life experience has been like, but you can suspend your judgement, get rid of any preconceived notions, and at least try putting yourself in their shoes for a while. Despite our differences, at the end of the day everybody essentially wants the same thing: to be understood, appreciated, and treated as equals. So, to that end, just remember the Golden Rule and do your best to treat others with the exact same kind of respect you would like them to show you. Let this be an overarching theme as you pursue meaningful connections and engage in all types of communication with your peers, instructors, and campus community members throughout your educational experience.

Engaging With Peers

Even a relatively small community college can seem like a big place if you grew up in a small town or attended a rural high school in a tight-knit community. Likewise, urban students can also feel disoriented in this setting, as they are more likely to be lacking in family, financial, and academic support for their college experience, just like their rural counterparts (Dennon, 2021). Regardless of your background, the college environment is just very different from high school and that can be a little scary at first. The lack of structure and the overall sense of freedom are favorable conditions and appropriate for adult education, but this unfamiliar academic setting can also be overwhelming and might make it seem more difficult to "find your place" on campus.

Thankfully, you are not alone. Regardless of your age, race, or economic background, most of us feel a little out of place at first. The best antidote to this condition is to find your tribe. Reaching out to your peers and making connections on campus will enrich your community college experience in multiple ways. It's also important to try to remain open and receptive on your end when others attempt to reach out to you. In this section, we'll explore the benefits of connecting with your fellow students in the classroom and on other parts of your campus.

Connecting in the Classroom (Formal Interactions)

One of the great features of the traditional face-to-face classroom setting is the direct, real-time human interaction you get to experience with your classmates (and your instructor). On the other hand, some students feel more comfortable interacting in the online classroom, where meaningful connections can also be made. Whichever type of learning environment you find yourself in, there are always valuable opportunities for making connections through interaction with your peers. Let's take a look at the nature of engagement opportunities in the classroom (face-to-face and online) and discuss why you should take advantage of them throughout your educational experience. We will label these classroom-based engagement activities as *formal* interactions.

Formal interactions would include any in-class or online activity that is built into the course and required by the instructor. Think mandatory discussion boards, group projects, or any other type of teamwork activity or collaboration in the classroom or online. Let's focus on the two major types of formal interactions you are likely to find on your campus.

Discussion boards are generally associated more with online courses, although they can also be used in traditional settings. This mode of interaction is often met with mixed reviews. While many argue that the general discussion board format needs more innovation or even major revision, other experts maintain that this tool can still provide a critical element of engagement and should not be discarded entirely (Lieberman, 2019).

Whatever the case may be, discussion boards remain the primary form of student interaction in online courses. They give you a voice to express your views and share your experiences while getting to know your peers a little better. In many cases, students may even prefer this type of interaction and feel compelled to engage in deeper levels of conversation than they would have in a face-to-face classroom. This may be partly because most students now communicate electronically through social media and email and feel more comfortable being open and expressing their opinions in the digital environment. Overall, this is a positive thing, because when students interact and feel a sense of belonging in their learning community, they are more likely to stick around and do well. In fact, research indicates that students with higher levels of engagement online tend to be more academically successful and personally satisfied with their courses (Shelton et al., 2017).

Group projects represent another type of formal interaction in the classroom setting. These can take a variety of forms and may last a single day or an entire semester. Group projects may involve working with one or several other students, depending on the nature of the project and the course you are in. Typical examples would be working with a partner in a science laboratory or working with a small group (three to five students) on some type of semester project that may culminate in a research paper or presentation. The second example of group work we just mentioned is quite common across many academic disciplines in the college setting. As instructors, we have seen it all in terms of student reactions to group work and the quality of the relationships and final products that emerge from these arrangements. Students can be uneasy about the concept of working as a team, especially if they are assigned to a group they did not choose. To be perfectly honest, the quality of your group project experience can depend on the members involved, but you can always control your actions and your attitude toward your group project and your fellow team members (recall the Mindset Mastery Tip **staying positive** from Chapter 1—that concept definitely applies here). On the other hand, many students like the idea of getting to work with their peers and dividing up the labor of an extensive project.

The truth is, whether you initially like the idea of group work or not, there is much to be gained from the experience of peer collaboration in a team environment. One primary skill (perhaps the most obvious) you can develop in a group is your teamwork ability. Teamwork activities in higher education can provide the same sense of purpose and motivation found in the workplace (Volkov & Volkov, 2015), and this is one of the most highly valued skills sought after by employers. You are very likely to encounter some type of question about your teamwork experience on employment applications or interviews, and nearly every job out there will require you to work in a group to achieve a common goal. Take note: in most cases you will probably *not* get to choose the group members on your team.

In addition to developing teamwork abilities, group project work can also enhance your ability to *think critically* and *communicate* with others. Furthermore, on a personal note, you may develop friendships with your group members and form a mutually beneficial academic partnership that extends beyond the scope of the project you all worked on. This is exactly what we will discuss in the next subsection. The "take home" point to remember is to try to be open and approach group project work with a positive attitude. This form of connecting in the classroom can benefit you in multiple ways, and if you can all come together and put in the right amount of effort, you can create something you can truly be proud of. Plus, it never hurts to score highly on a project that may be worth a large chunk of your grade.

Connecting Outside of the Classroom (Informal Interactions)

Informal interactions will be defined here as any type of voluntary student collaboration outside of the classroom for academic or social benefit. We will discuss two major types of informal interactions in this subsection: study groups and student organizations.

Study groups involve communicating and working with classmates on course-related content outside of the classroom when it is not required by the instructor. These arrangements can be highly effective in terms of learning course content, connecting with your peers, and holding yourself accountable for studying. Group study or tutoring sessions may be organized and offered by the college, but independent, informal student-led sessions are also very common and effective. Students who study together in groups may learn faster and gain a greater understanding of the content through interaction with their peers, who bring different insights and perspectives to the table. In addition, study group individuals tend to be more motivated to study considering they have some level of commitment to the group and likely look forward to meeting up with others for educational and social reasons.

A recent study showed that the top three strategies utilized in study groups were asking each other questions about the content, discussing course material in depth, and quizzing each other—all of which are evidence-based strategies (McCabe & Lummis, 2018). The majority of students in the study reported they felt their level of learning increased compared to studying alone and almost 70% said that being in the study group increased their motivation to study. What's more impressive is the data showed students who engaged more often in deep content reflection, making flashcards, and holding shorter but more frequent study sessions had higher GPAs than others in the study. With the results of this study in mind, the following recommendations can be followed to optimize study group effectiveness (Weimer, 2018):

- **Keep the group small** (three to five students max, otherwise it can be hard to keep everyone on the same page).
- **Meet more often but for shorter periods of time** (this concept is called "spacing," and it's better for knowledge retention and to avoid last-minute cramming).
- **Prepare an agenda and expect group members to come prepared** (this goes back to the whole accountability thing and will make for much more productive sessions).

- **Use good study strategies** (explain things to each other, ask questions, work through problems together to understand—not just memorize—the content).

Once again, this type of student interaction also has a social component to it that can enhance your overall college experience. Group study sessions can take place on campus, but you can also meet at your local coffee shop, restaurant, or internet café. As long as you have an environment that allows for effective communication, there is nothing wrong with a little change in scenery every once in a while. And while these study groups are great for getting through an isolated course (especially a difficult one), you may establish a group with others of the same major that could carry you all successfully through the entire program. In this kind of long-term support group, you might be surprised by the lasting friendships that may result.

Student organizations are another great way to connect with peers on your campus. Even though they typically don't have a direct impact on academic success, these organizations can create a strong sense of community, and students who feel engaged and involved on their campus are more likely to stick around and succeed. In Chapter 2, you were asked to research the student clubs or organizations on your campus and to indicate any you may be interested in joining. Outside of a student government association, the organizations on a community college can vary widely from one campus to the next. Because of the campus-specific and unique nature of these clubs and organizations, we won't spend much time attempting to describe all the possible types here. That being said, any club or organization at your college would probably add value to your experience and the possibilities are certainly worth exploring. Whether you're into science or engineering, creative writing, drama, health care occupations, foreign languages, education, criminal justice, or other fields, odds are there is an organization on campus that would suit your interest.

There is one established two-year college organization we should mention by name, as it is very widespread and potentially very beneficial to those who join its ranks. **Phi Theta Kappa** (PTK), the official student honor society for community colleges, has been around for over 100 years and boasts more than 3.5 million members from the United States and around the

Activity 4.1 *Student Interaction Reflection*

Following our discussion on interacting with your peers on campus, let's take a moment to pause and reflect on any experiences you've had so far and what you might anticipate gaining in future collaborations with your classmates in various possible settings.

On a separate sheet of paper or in the space provided below, answer the following questions to help reflect on your experiences and expectations with regard to student interactions.

1. List any experiences you've had in college or high school that involved group projects, study groups, or participation in any kind of student club or organization.

(*Continued*)

Activity 4.1 (*Continued*)

2. Which experiences were your favorite and why? Did you benefit from them academically, personally, or both?

3. Considering your current (or prospective) major at the college, in which courses do you think forming an informal, student-led study group would be beneficial?

4. Do you feel you would benefit from a long-term study group interaction in your major program? Briefly explain why or why not (no wrong answers here).

globe. The organization is meant to give high-performing students the recognition they deserve and provide them with support through scholarship opportunities and other means. For more information on PTK and to see if your campus has a chapter, visit their website at ptk.org.

Communicating With Instructors

One of the biggest mistakes students can make, especially early on in their college career, is *not* communicating effectively with their instructor. If you are unsure about which textbook to purchase, you should ask your instructor. If you feel completely lost after the first week of lecture even after studying the material outside of class, you should let your instructor know. If you are ill or have to miss class for some other reason, you should notify your instructor as soon as you can and ask them *what* you missed (not *if* you missed anything—trust us on this one) and if there's anything you can do to make up a missed assignment or get caught up with the material.

If you experience any of the issues just described, or others like them, it's always better for you *and* for your instructor to address them immediately.

Success Tip

What we're getting at here is there's a balance in the student-instructor relationship: both parties have certain responsibilities they must fulfill in order to maximize the chances of a successful course experience. You, the *student*, are responsible for showing up, getting informed about the course (read the syllabus!) and keeping up with the schedule, putting in the required study effort to succeed, and notifying your instructor as soon as any issues arise. Your *instructor* should be patient, available and willing to help, as clear and informative as possible, and understanding and flexible when extreme personal circumstances in a student's life call for it.

The longer you wait, the more difficult it may become for your instructor to get you back on the right path, so let them know about any difficulties you are having as soon as possible. Remember that your instructor is on your side—they want you to succeed! And if they've been teaching for any length of time, they should be well aware of how much students need their support to navigate the course. It's no surprise that instructor support is one of the most highly valued elements of the college classroom, and a strong predictor for student satisfaction in the online learning environment (Keeney et al., 2017).

Since this book is not written for instructors and, of course, you can only control your own actions and attitude in these settings, we will focus solely on what you can do to communicate effectively with your instructor. On a side note, however, if you believe you are genuinely being treated unfairly, you may consider contacting their superior (the appropriate department chair or dean) or voicing your concerns on the course evaluation that usually goes out to students toward the end of the semester. These evaluations do get read by administrators, so your voice will be heard, and actions may be taken. On the flip side, positive evaluations are also noted by administration. This is a great way to repay the favor if you really enjoyed your instructor or your experience in a particular course.

Instructor Email Etiquette 101

Although you are certainly encouraged to call your instructor or set up an office appointment to discuss any issues, the reality is probably more than 90% of student-instructor communication outside of the classroom now takes place via email. Because this mode of communication is so dominant in our increasingly digital society, we will spend the remainder of this section discussing how to properly send an email to your professor. We'll begin with a list of pointers on what to do, and what *not* to do, when communicating by this method, and finish with a hands-on application of these tips in Activity 4.2.

Consider the list below as your general guidelines for emailing your instructor:

1. **Send the message from your official college email account (not personal email account).** This will help the instructor identify who you are and see that you are familiar with the official channel of communication for all course-related emails and announcements.

2. **Formally greet the instructor.** A simple "Good morning" or even just "Hello" goes a long way at the beginning of an email, and if they have a doctoral degree, go ahead and address them as "Dr." (the Dr. title may not matter as much to some, but it's better to be on the safe side and show respect).

3. **State your name and the course name and your course section.** It's extremely important to identify yourself and the exact class section in which you are enrolled. Nearly all of your instructors teach multiple courses, and many (if not most) will teach multiple sections of the same course. Don't make them have to guess or track you down to figure out which course and section you are referring to. They are busy and receive way more student emails than you might think, especially during peak times in the semester.

4. **If asking a question, be as specific as possible.** Try not to just say something like "I'm lost, please help." State what it is that you are stuck on and indicate any study efforts you have made on your own to learn the concept so far. This will make it much easier for the instructor to understand the problem and actually provide the help you are needing.

5. **Check the syllabus and course schedule first for the answer!** It's not that instructors don't like to confirm or help out if you are unclear on something, but if you ask about something simple that is clearly stated in the syllabus or schedule, it can be frustrating for the instructor. Again, we don't mind helping at all, just don't skip straight to emailing first for questions without even bothering to read the course materials. Believe it or not, instructors put *a lot* of time and effort into designing all point values, grading and submission policies, and due dates for a course. Most of us spend hours even just adjusting the assignments and creating a schedule for a new semester. But, as we said, for more serious issues you are truly confused about (or even just a little unclear on) after doing your part to investigate, do not hesitate to contact your instructor.

6. **Avoid using obscure slang, acronyms, or being too informal.** Common acronyms such as "ty" (thank you) or "tia" (thanks in advance) may be meaningless to your instructor and indicate a general lack of effort in your message. Remember, you are not texting your friends, and it's best to avoid this type of language so that your instructor does not make assumptions about your level of commitment to the course.

7. **Close with a "thank you" and your name.** Again, this is a courtesy thing and just a general show of respect that you took the time to say "thank you" or something of that nature and sign off with your name. If you already stated your full name in the email, first name only should be fine here at the end.

Activity 4.2 *The Perfect Instructor Email*

Okay, so maybe "perfect" is a bit of a stretch, but let's try and apply *all* of the guidelines we just learned and craft an ideal email to your instructor. If at all possible, try to practice with an actual question or issue you may need to ask any of your instructors at this very moment. You may also use a past question you had or anticipate a future question or issue that may come up. Be sure and address all seven guidelines, above. You can draft this on paper or in your actual email system and take a screenshot to submit or show to your instructor for credit.

End-of-Chapter Questions

1. **Recall.** Define *formal* and *informal* interactions with your peers on campus and give examples of each. What is the major difference between these two types? What are some

general benefits of working in study groups? Name some evidence-based strategies and techniques you can apply in these arrangements.

2. **Engage.** Partner up and connect with at least one other classmate who comes from a background different than your own with regard to gender, race, religion, or place of residence. Come up with a list of three to five questions to ask them related to their upbringing, cultural background, or general interests (can be anything from family traditions, religious affiliation, favorite activities, books, music, TV series, etc.). Document your classmate's responses in four to six sentences.
3. **Reflect.** Consider the Success Tip related to the balance in student-instructor relationship. In a 100-word response, provide an honest reflection on your commitments to the student responsibilities described and discuss the degree to which your instructor (can be any of your instructors) held up their end of the deal in this balance (or failed to do so).
4. **Create.** In Activity 4.2, we attempted to craft the "perfect" instructor email. Now let's do the opposite! Compose a very poorly written email to an instructor, breaking as many of the guideline rules as possible. Have some fun and be as inappropriate as possible without being vulgar or profane. Share with another classmate and see if they can identify how many guidelines you destroyed in the process!

References

Dennon, A. (2021, January 21). College attendance among rural students takes a dive [Blog post]. *Best Colleges*. https://www.bestcolleges.com/blog/rural-students-college-enrollment-decline/

Keeney, H. E., Shelton, V. K., Mason, D. M., & Young, J. K. (2017). DELES analysis of E-learning environments: Satisfaction guaranteed? In K. Shelton & K. Peterson (Eds.), *Handbook of research on building, growing, and sustaining quality E-Learning programs* (pp. 128–150). IGI Global.

Lieberman, M. (2019, March 27). *Discussion boards: Valuable? Overused? Discuss.* Inside Higher Ed. https://www.insidehighered.com/digital-learning/article/2019/03/27/new-approaches-discussion-boards-aim-dynamic-online-learning

McCabe, J. A., & Lummis, S. N. (2018). Why and how do undergraduates study in groups? *Scholarships of Teaching and Learning in Psychology, 4*(1), 27–42.

National Center for Education Statistics. (2022, May). *Racial/Ethnic Enrollment in Public Schools.* https://nces.ed.gov/programs/coe/indicator/cge

Shelton, B. E., Hung, J. L., & Lowenthal, P. R. (2017). Predicting student success by modeling student interaction in asynchronous online courses. *Distance Education, 38*(1), 59–69. https://doi.org/10.1080/01587919.2017.1299562

Volkov, A., & Volkov, M. (2015). Teamwork benefits in tertiary education: Student perceptions that lead to best practice assessment design. *Education and Training, 57*(3), 262–278. https://doi.org/10.1108/ET-02-2013-0025

Weimer, M. (2018, May 16). *The benefits of study groups.* Faculty Focus. https://www.facultyfocus.com/articles/course-design-ideas/what-students-can-learn-from-studying-together/

Image Credits

IMG 4.1: Copyright © 2017 Depositphotos/ArturVerkhovetskiy.

CHAPTER 5

Staying the Course

Committing to Your Classes and Learning to Study Your Way

Image 5.1

Introduction

Welcome to the second half of your course journey! We are now just past the halfway point in our semester, but you'll have many more semesters to go before your academic journey comes to an end. As amazing and rewarding the as the college experience is, there is no doubt that it can be a grind—both mentally and physically. To succeed on your higher education journey, you have to commit to the process and work extremely hard, often for a number of years. In other words, you have to stay the course. This involves a lot of class attendance and a whole lot of studying, but of course it's all worth it in the end. In Chapter 5, we'll explore the following themes:

- The importance of attendance and why it matters to show up and commit to your classes
- Getting to know your learning style and how it can influence the way you study
- Tips and techniques for how to study effectively for your classes

Here's a brief summary of the main sections contained in Chapter 5: In "Why Attendance Matters," we explore the topic of attendance in greater detail, pointing out the top three reasons why it matters and viewing your thoughts on the topic in Activity 5.1—Your Thoughts on Attendance. "Knowing Your Learning Style" takes a look at different learning styles based on your personality type and suggests how this characteristic might impact the study techniques that work best for you. "Study Tips and Techniques: 5 Key Practices" presents five effective tools for how to approach studying for content mastery on exams and concludes with Activity 5.2—Your Study Habits.

Endurance is one of the most difficult disciplines, but it is to the one who endures that the final victory comes.

—Gautama Buddha

Why Attendance Matters

As you may notice, several recurring themes will continue to emerge throughout our textbook. Attendance is certainly one of them, and for good reason. Recall in the previous chapter we talked at length about the importance of making connections in college through interaction with your peers and your instructors. Clearly, these connections cannot be made and developed further if you don't show up for class (or participate in the online environment). We also mentioned attendance in Chapter 3, highlighting that it appears to be a key variable in predicting academic success. In this section, we'll go over several specific reasons to pinpoint just why attendance is so important. But first, let's see what you think about the topic.

Activity 5.1 *Your Thoughts on Attendance*

Instructions: In the space provided or on a separate sheet of paper, make a quick list of all the ways that you think attendance can affect your course performance. You can list the benefits of attending class and/or the negative effects of not attending. Let's make this a quick activity. You have three minutes ... Go!

Phew, what a rush, huh? Hopefully this got your wheels turning on the reasons why you value attendance, or at least how it can impact your success in a course and, ultimately, your community college experience. Now let's lay out and explore the top three reasons for making the effort to show up to class. Take note on any of these that made your list in the previous activity.

1. **It's a sign of respect.** Showing up for class on a consistent basis signals respect not only to your instructor, but to your classmates as well. You all are in this together and need each other not only for group work assignments, but also just to give a sense of emotional support—you *all* add value to the learning community just by showing up and being present. On that note, do your best to actually be present and attentive in the class. Act like you want to be there and that you value this experience as an important part of your life (because it is!). Believe, me this goes a *long* way with your instructor, who also very

much appreciates the engagement and support. These individuals work very hard putting themselves out there every class period to try to create a positive, productive learning space. It's not easy, folks. Finally, this shows respect for yourself. College is a personal journey and how it turns out is up to you. Show that you care about your future and your academic legacy by showing up and putting your best foot forward.

2. **You won't miss valuable information.** This is a big one. When you miss even one class, you usually miss a lot. Here's a short list of critical items you could be missing by not showing up for class:
   - **Lecture content.** (This one's pretty obvious.)
   - **Test information.** (Dates, key areas to study, test design, etc.—these things can change from the way they were originally planned, plus it's just good to be reminded of when the test is coming up.)
   - **The dreaded pop quiz!** (Not everyone's favorite activity, but you don't want to miss out on those points. Nothing to fear if you've been attending and engaging with the content.)
   - **Participation points.** (Instructors often attach point values to in-class activities or even attendance itself.)
3. **You will absorb the content.** If you show up to class and pay attention, the exposure to and engagement with the lecture content will add up in your favor. This kind of routine repetition helps your brain to process and solidify the lessons you will be tested on in the near future. As we mentioned in Chapter 3, this is an extremely valuable and beneficial use of your time. Being more familiar with the content will make studying for the exam much less of a burden and increase your chances for success.

Success Tip

One more good reason why it's important to show up to class regularly, on time, and to stay engaged while you're there: reference letters. Whatever field you are going into, it's almost a certainty that at some point you will need a reference letter for a job application, internship, or maybe even scholarship. Your past (or current) instructors are an excellent source for providing these letters. And if you showed up to class, worked hard, and conducted yourself with integrity, your instructor will have zero problems giving an honest assessment of why you deserve serious consideration as a candidate for this job, internship, scholarship, et cetera. As instructors, we have all had multiple reference letters written on our behalf and certainly don't mind returning the favor *if* the student has earned our respect. We love bragging on our students and welcome the opportunity to help them out beyond the borders of the classroom!

Knowing Your Learning Style

Before we take a look at some actual techniques for studying, let us consider a few personality factors that may influence your way of studying—that is, the studying style that works best for you. The idea that people exhibit different learning styles has been around since at least the 1970s, and since then, learning style theories have had a major impact on the field of education (Moayyeri, 2015). These theories are generally rooted in the idea that different people approach and respond to learning information in different ways. Therefore, it may be helpful to understand how you learn best and use this information to adjust your study strategies accordingly to keep you interested and engaged.

Most learning style theories are based on the ideas of Carl Jung (1875–1961), the famous Swiss psychologist credited with the establishment of analytical psychology. Jung theorized that people can generally be categorized based on four different personality types (Cherry, 2020):

1. **Introversion vs. Extraversion**
2. **Sensation vs. Intuition**
3. **Thinking vs. Feeling**
4. **Judging vs. Perceiving**

Let's take a quick look at how each of these personality types may affect your approach to studying for quizzes and exams.

- ***Introverted*** learners like to work alone in quiet reflection, and prefer to listen, watch, and observe others before attempting a new skill. ***Extraverted*** learners learn best through direct experience, enjoy working in groups, and are willing to lead, participate, offer opinions, and jump into an activity without guidance from others.
- ***Sensing*** learners observe the surrounding world, focus on the present, and use common sense and experience to solve problems, whereas ***intuitive*** learners appreciate new challenges and experiences, and prefer to view the "big picture" when exploring theories and abstract ideas.
- ***Thinking*** learners base their decisions on reason and logic and tend to avoid or exclude emotional factors from their process. ***Feeling*** learners are more in tune with their emotions and those of the people around them. They base their decisions on immediate feelings and may generate excitement or enthusiasm in group settings.
- ***Judging*** learners tend to be organized, structured, and firm in their decisions. They dislike unknown or ambiguous scenarios, have strong opinions, and generally follow the rules. ***Perceiving*** learners make impulsive decisions, will change their stances based on new information, and may have trouble making decisions, in general. They tend to be flexible and adaptable and dislike structure and organization.

Surely, you can see some of your own personality traits in Jung's ideas, presented above, and this knowledge alone can help you tailor a study routine that suits your needs. Note that you may very well be some combination of the traits described and these can certainly change or evolve through time. There is absolutely nothing wrong with this, and there is no right or wrong way to be when it comes to how you prefer to study or process information. If you do wish to explore this concept further and dig into the type of learning style that describes you best, then you are in luck, my friend. There are multiple questionnaires or learning inventories that have been designed specifically for that purpose. Here's one of the most popular questionnaires that's available for free online:

- The **VARK** (**V**isual, **A**ural, **R**ead/write, **K**inesthetic) Questionnaire: https://vark-learn.com/the-vark-questionnaire/

Study Tips and Techniques: 5 Key Practices

Once the college experience begins, students may find in many cases that the level of coursework is a whole new ball game compared to high school. As a natural progression, courses at the college level are more advanced, requiring a deeper investigation into the subject matter. This means the level of difficulty increases and your study skills need to be developed and improved upon in order to keep pace. With that goal in mind, this section will cover five key practices for you to experiment with. These practices are a mix of tips on how to approach studying and actual study techniques to help step up your game. Remember that based on your learning style, some of these techniques may work better for you than others.

The key thing, no matter which techniques you prefer, is to *keep going*. Put in the work and find out what is most effective for you. You have to find the motivation to dive into your courses, study hard, and keep studying (even when more attractive options present themselves). This is what the title of this chapter is pointing out: you have to *stay the course* and keep working hard in order to succeed in college. In the next chapter, we will look at various test-taking strategies, but none of these will help you if you don't put in the study time beforehand. There is simply no substitute for consistent, effective studying if you want to do well on exams. So let's take a look now at five key practices that can help you study better and succeed on test day.

1. **Test Yourself.** Rather than simply reading over or highlighting your notes or the textbook, begin testing yourself by answering practice questions as early as possible. Even if you don't know the content well at all yet, working through actual questions will help you learn the material. And what better way to prepare yourself for the real thing? Your textbook should always provide practice questions, and if your instructor provides any kind of study guide or practice test, absolutely pay close attention to these and work through them as much as possible. Finally, don't be afraid to create your own questions. Obviously, you will know the answers, but going through this exercise can help wrap your mind around the material and you may even be able to anticipate the kinds of questions your instructor will ask on exam day.

2. **Study With Intense Focus.** With all the distractions in our lives (social media, family, work issues, etc.), it can be very difficult to sit down, focus, and do nothing but study the content. This means no scrolling on your phone, no listening to a podcast or streaming Netflix in the background, and not letting your mind wander through different topics. A little light music in the background might be okay, depending on your personal preference and attention span, but it's generally not recommended if it distracts you from the material. Again, it can be challenging to stay in this zone, but it's worth it from a time

investment perspective if nothing else. It's been suggested that one hour of an intensely focused study session—one with absolute minimal distractions—results in the same level of effectiveness as three hours of studying with distractions (Kang, 2019)!

3. **Space Out Your Study Times.** Studying in short, intensely focused sessions over time is highly preferred to marathon cramming sessions. After a certain amount of time, it becomes difficult (if not impossible) to remain focused and study effectively. Your mind can process and retain information much better if you take in the content in shorter more intentional segments. Keep in mind that in order to do this the right way, you have to start studying early on in the semester—ideally from the very beginning. This is exactly why we say to study early and often rather than late and out of desperation.
4. **Create Your Own Study Materials.** In addition to writing your own questions, there are multiple types of study materials you can create to get directly involved with the learning process and reinforce the concepts you are trying to master. This technique comes with several benefits. The act of making them is a creative process that enhances critical thinking, you will be reviewing and learning the content in the process of making them, and after they're made you now have a great tool to practice studying with. Here's a short list of materials you can make on your own:
   - ***Flashcards***—A classic study material, but still a popular and effective option to use. These can be done the old-fashioned way (on paper) or digitally through the use of new software programs.
   - ***Concept maps***—Also called "mind maps," these tools are a great way to summarize a topic (or several) and connect the different elements of it to add detail and show how various elements relate to one another. These maps can take various forms and may be created for any topic or subject. For a few good examples of concept maps, check here: https://learningcenter.unc.edu/tips-and-tools/using-concept-maps/.
   - ***Concept tables***—A slightly less visual, more structured version of the concept map would be a concept table. This would involve a different design using rows and columns to input detailed information on related topics. Laying all the content out like this in table format can make it easier to visualize, understand, and retain.
   - ***Topic summary***—Let's say you have a topic in biology or an event in history that you will need to understand thoroughly on an exam. One way to check (and enhance) your understanding is to write it down in your own words. Pretend like you had to explain or teach it to someone else who has no knowledge of the topic. Make it as clear as possible in your own mind by repeating this process until you get it right. Note that this is a great way to prepare for essay questions.
5. **Study in Groups.** In Chapter 4, when discussing engaging with peers, we laid out several suggestions for how to pursue group work and why it's beneficial. Remember that working with others can help you uncover gaps in your own understanding that may be revealed by your classmates. It's beneficial to view the content through the different perspectives

your study group brings, and explaining your take on a concept can also help to organize and reinforce your own views of a topic. Finally, study groups are the perfect place for sharing study materials with others and practice by quizzing each other on the course topics.

Getting to Know Dr. K: Positive Growth Through Group Study

Hey, friends! Dr. K here with one more quick plug for the value of studying with others. Many of you may have read the introvert learning style description in this chapter and thought "yep, that's me." There's nothing wrong with this and, in fact, your most intensely focused study sessions probably need to be alone to minimize distraction. On a personal level, I definitely identified with the introvert personality, especially when I was younger, and on some level I still do. When I started college, I kept to myself and avoided informal study sessions with others unless it was somehow required in the course. Then over time, I changed my habits. It wasn't really a conscious or deliberate decision and it didn't happen all at once, but now when I think back to my courses later in college, I had formed or joined informal "self-made" study groups in just about every one of my classes. The results of this changed my college experience on several levels—all of them positive. I felt more of an obligation to show up for class *and* to study, because my group was counting on me. I became more engaged in my courses and on campus and had some really great times with some cool people in the process—all of them trying to succeed in the course just like I was. So beyond the academic benefit, I would strongly encourage you to leave your comfort zone and reach out to others for support. Opening yourself up in this way can enhance the social and relationship dimension, which is a huge part of your college experience. You may even make some good memories and lasting friendships in the process!

Activity 5.2 *Your Study Habits*

Instructions: In the space provided or on a separate sheet of paper, provide a brief response (three to four sentences) to the questions, below, related to your study habits.

1. What are your current study habits? Describe the length of time and frequency for your typical study sessions, and list any specific practices or techniques you currently use.

2. Describe any ways you think you could improve your study habits (be specific), and list any tips or techniques from this chapter that you may incorporate into your future study practice.

End-of-Chapter Questions

1. **Recall.** List the top three reasons (from the chapter) for why attendance matters. Name the Swiss psychologist whose ideas created the basis for most learning style theories. List several reasons why creating your own study materials can be beneficial.
2. **Engage.** Pair up with a classmate or form a small group and discuss your current study habits, sharing any current tips or strategies you are using. Document your classmate's responses in four to six sentences.
3. **Reflect.** In a 100-word response, reflect on your personality type based on the descriptions above from the ideas of Carl Jung. Describe how you think this might affect your learning style and which techniques are most effective for you.
4. **Create.** Choose a chapter in this book (or any book) and draw your own concept map for the topic. Be sure to draw lines to connect the concepts within the topic and show the relationships between them.

References

Cherry, K. (2020, May 9). *Learning styles based on Jung's theory of personality.* Verywellmind.com. https://www.verywellmind.com/jungs-theory-of-personality-learning-styles-2795160

Kang, E. (2019, April 4). *5 research-backed studying techniques.* Edutopia. https://www.edutopia.org/article/5-research-backed-studying-techniques

Moayyeri, H. (2015). The impact of undergraduate students' learning preferences (VARK Model) on their language achievement. *Journal of Language Teaching and Research, 6*(1), 132–139.

Image Credits

IMG 5.1: Copyright © 2020 Depositphotos/moviafilmes.

CHAPTER 6

Remembering to Breathe

The Strategic Art of Taking (and Acing) Exams

Image 6.1

Introduction

Whether we like it or not, taking exams is a big part of the college experience and often constitutes the majority of your course grade. Of course, the studying you do leading up to the exam is critical; however, there are also steps you can take before and during the test to increase your chances for a successful outcome. In Chapter 6, we'll explore the following themes:

- Preparing for exams using techniques beyond actual studying
- General test-taking strategies to apply right before, during, and right after taking an exam
- Learning how to approach exam questions based on the question type.

Here's a brief summary of the main sections contained in Chapter 6: In "Be Prepared: Test Preparation Techniques," we'll cover several techniques (outside of studying) you can employ before taking the exam and explore your impressions of the topic in Activity 6.1—Test Preparation Techniques: Your Initial Thoughts. "General Test-Taking Strategies" reviews several strategies you can use right before, during, and right after an exam, laid out in Table 6.1. Finally, the last section of the chapter, "The Variety of Exam Questions: What to Expect and How to Approach Them," provides guidance and strategies on how to effectively approach the five most common question types you will likely encounter on exams.

Breath is the bridge which connects life to consciousness,
which unites your body to your thoughts.
—Thich Nhat Hanh

Be Prepared: Test Preparation Techniques

Test taking. Arguably one of the most stressful activities one can engage in, especially during your college years. At times, it can be right up there with, say, getting a root canal on local anesthetic or maybe skydiving but without all the thrill. Even if you've done your homework, studied adequately, and feel that you have a pretty firm grasp on the material, sitting down in that classroom (or in front of your computer) to take an exam can fill your mind with anxiety and self-doubt. The reasons for this are not unfounded. Let's face it, it can be difficult to know what to expect and sometimes there may be a lot on the line. This is exactly why it's so important to do everything you can to prepare for the experience and cut down on unwanted stress as much as possible.

No need to fear—we're here to help! There's no perfect "one-size-fits-all" solution that works for everyone, but if you experiment with the techniques outlined in this section—and this chapter—you can greatly increase your chances for success on exams, and hopefully decrease your heart rate and blood pressure in the process. In this section, we're going to address the importance of test preparation. The previous chapter focused mainly on study techniques, and it remains true that there is absolutely no way around it: if you don't put in the work and appropriate amount of study time, you will be at a distinct disadvantage on the test. However, that's not all we mean here by preparation. There are other things that you can (and should) do before an exam to increase your chances for success. We're going to spend the rest of this section describing two broad areas of test preparation techniques, but first let's dive into a quick activity to see how *you* think you should prepare. Consider it a test ☺.

Activity 6.1 *Test Preparation Techniques: Your Initial Thoughts*

Before we actually get into the practical techniques in this section, take a moment to express any thoughts or ideas you may have other than studying that could help you prepare for exams. Unlike a real test, there are no wrong answers here. This is just an exercise to gauge your current knowledge and experience on the topic.

(*Continued*)

Activity 6.1 (*Continued*)

Instructions: In the space provided or on a separate sheet of paper, provide a list or brief response for each item below. For each answer you give, specify if this is something you've actually done or just something you think would help.

1. Imagine you have a test coming up next week. Try to list at least five questions you would ask your instructor about the test, assuming you don't know any details about it at this point other than the basic content you have covered.

2. List any other test preparation techniques you can think of. This can include anything (besides studying or asking questions about the exam).

Okay, that was fun. Hopefully, it at least got you thinking about things you have done or could do (outside of studying) to put yourself in the best possible position to have a successful test experience. For the remainder of this section, let's go through some practical techniques you can apply to get ready for any test you might be taking.

Test Preparation Techniques: Practical Tips for Success

In this subsection we'll present two broad test preparation techniques and dive into each of them in detail. Although these techniques do involve study habits in some cases, many aspects of them go outside and beyond the act of studying. Let's take a look at what you can do to increase your chances for success.

1. **Ask Questions.** So we kind of gave this one away in Activity 6.1, but let's take a closer look and list some test preparation questions you may not have thought of during the activity. To clarify, these are actually questions you should ask yourself before the test. If you can't definitively answer these questions based on your notes or the course information provided (i.e., syllabus and schedule) or you're just not quite sure, then you should *definitely* consult your instructor for the answers as soon as possible or at least a week before the exam.

Here's a pretest checklist of questions to make sure you're prepared for any exam:

- **What is the exact date and time of the test?** This one seems obvious, but the fact is students miss tests all the time or get caught off guard when the test "sneaks up" before they are ready. Get *all* test dates down as soon as possible. Write them on your planner or calendar and keep a close eye on them throughout the semester. If the test is online during a certain window of time, make sure you know exactly when that window opens and, more importantly, when the test closes.

- **What is the time limit?** In a face-to-face classroom, the test is generally the full length of the class period, but online it's extremely important to know how long you have and to keep a close eye on your pace and the time remaining for completion.

- **How many questions will there be?** This is good to know as it helps you to mentally envision the test beforehand, and it's very important for setting and keeping your pace for getting done on time.

- **What types of questions will be on the test and how many of each?** This is very good to know, especially before the first exam, and it helps to know this as early in the semester as possible. Once again, this will help you form a mental picture of how the test will look, and it will influence how you practice (aka study) before the exam. (In the next section, we'll look at the various types of exam questions you may possibly encounter in more detail and provide tips on how to approach them.)

- **How many points are the questions worth?** It's important to know the point value of each question and each type of question. This will also help you prepare and anticipate which areas you should pay extra attention to, both before and during the test.

- **How much is the test worth, relative to the entire course grade?** Are all tests valued the same or are some worth more than others? Also, what percentage of the entire course grade does the test count for? You need to know exactly how much of your total course grade is at stake each and every time you begin an exam. This can give a sense of just how important the test is and help motivate you to take it seriously and prepare as much as possible.

- **Is there a "dropped" exam or exam replacement policy?** It's not too uncommon for an instructor to drop your lowest exam score or maybe replace your lowest regular exam score with the final exam grade. If such a policy is in place, this should *not* encourage you to take the exam lightly or slack in your preparation! But it is somewhat reassuring to know that if you don't do well, there's still an opportunity to make up for it later on. Anything that adds to your sense of calmness and mental clarity going into an exam is definitely a good thing.

- **What is the best way to prepare?** Kind of a vague, open-ended question, but one that is worth asking. Yes, this does tie in to studying, but it's also a question you should ask before any test you take. Obviously, if there's any kind of review sheet, study guide, or practice test, you should be all over it. Instructors put these together for a reason, so pay close attention and make sure you are comfortable with the material *and* the related content! In other words, don't just memorize the exact questions and answers from a study guide or practice test—make sure you have a broad understanding of the concepts surrounding these questions and be prepared to answer other questions that are related to these concepts. Even if there are no formal test review materials provided, your instructor may still be able to tell you which concepts to make sure to focus on, and they may even provide some tips on how to practice for certain types of questions. And don't forget, you can always use this kind of information to *create your own study guide* or review materials, as we discussed in the previous chapter.

Success Tip

As you can see from the nature of the questions in the pretest checklist, we are trying our best to form as complete and clear a picture of the exam as possible before actually going in to take it. When you have a vision for what the test will look like, this will help you strategize and prepare, and it will give you a sense of familiarity and even comfort, since you know (for the most part) what to expect. This comfort level can lead to increased confidence and enable you to start thinking positively toward your goal of a successful test experience. This goes all the way back to the mastering your mindset concept we explored in Chapter 1. Believe in yourself, picture a positive result in your mind, then go make it happen! If you've put in the work studying beforehand and follow the techniques offered in this chapter, it should be well within your grasp in most cases.

2. **Take Care of Yourself: Reducing Test Anxiety.** We've already established that test taking can be a stressful ordeal, and at this point in your academic career, you probably don't need any person or textbook to tell you that. Going into a test with an overstressed mind or body is not ideal for academic performance. This is why it's important to do as much as you can to reduce **test anxiety**—that nervous feeling you get leading up to a test and while taking it.

   Test anxiety can affect children or adults at all levels of education, but it seems to be a bit more serious at the college level, where the stakes tend to be higher. A low level of test anxiety is perfectly normal and may even help sharpen your mind and focus your attention. However, too much anxiety can make you miserable and negatively affect your performance on a test (Sawchuk, 2017). The good news is, there are steps you can take to help yourself out in this area. In fact, research has shown that learning certain techniques, such as relaxation methods and test-taking skills, can significantly reduce test anxiety in college students (Wachelka & Katz, 1999). Here are some techniques you can try, in no particular order:

   - **Remember to breathe.** Breathing and meditation techniques can calm your mind and relax the body, both of which can help get you in the right state of mind to do your best on test day. Slow, conscious breathing right before and even during the exam can also help keep you calm and focused.

- **Eat healthy and hydrate.** Your body and mind are definitely related, so do your best to take care of both by fueling up with good food and drinking plenty of water. A little coffee or tea is generally fine, but be careful with excessive sugar, caffeine, or energy drinks. These things can cause your body to crash at inconvenient times and may actually increase anxiety.
- **Get active.** Exercise and physical activity are great ways to release tension. They can also help you sleep better and provide a break from studying, allowing your brain to process and integrate the material you are learning.
- **Get sleep.** Even adults need an adequate amount of quality sleep in order to perform their best, academically. Low sleep can make you tired, irritable, and mentally cloudy, making it harder to recall all the information you've worked so hard to retain. This is yet another reason why we advise against cramming before a test.
- **Study consistently.** When preparing for an exam, your study *techniques* are certainly important (see Chapter 5), but so are your study *habits*. We have certainly touched on this before, but it's worth repeating here in the context of this particular chapter. Studying early and often (rather than cramming at the last minute) will make you more familiar and comfortable with the test material, leading to increased self-confidence and an optimistic outlook leading up to the exam.
- **Set a routine.** Any type of pretest ritual (including those related to the items above) can help to set your mind at ease before a big exam. This can include any number of personal activities you routinely do the night before and/or the day of the test. The idea is not to be superstitious; it's more about doing familiar activities that can be reassuring and put you in a good headspace before your test.
- **Talk to your classmates.** It's always a good idea to run your perceptions of and expectations for a test by your classmates for feedback. There's a chance you could be missing out on important information or details that others may have. Also, it's just good to build a sense of community knowing that you're all in it together. This is the same basic supportive function you can find in a study group.
- **Don't ignore a disability.** Test anxiety can be a problem for anyone, but for those with learning issues or disabilities, it can be crippling to academic performance. If you think you may be experiencing a learning disorder that is affecting your ability to read or remain focused, do not hesitate to contact the disability services department at your institution for possible assistance. Their sole purpose is helping students in need.

General Test-Taking Strategies

Before we jump into specific strategies for answering the different types of questions you may encounter on an exam, let's take a moment to cover some general strategies that apply right before, during, and right after taking a test.

Table 6.1 presents a list of general test-taking strategies to consider, adapted from North Shore Community College (n.d.):

Table 6.1

When you do it	Strategy	Why you do it
Right before the test	Glance over the entire test.	Helps to get an overall feel for the length of the test and the different sections it contains.
	Read *all* instructions carefully.	To make sure you understand exactly what you are required to do for all sections of the test.
	Calculate your pace for answering questions.	Always good to stay on track so you can finish on time. You can do this ahead of time if you have all the details on the number/type of questions. *(Ex: If you have 50 questions and 60 minutes, try to answer around one question per minute and know that you need to be about halfway done at the 30-minute mark.)*
During the test	Read *all* questions carefully.	To make sure you are clearly reading every question and know exactly what it's asking. Be careful to not assume you recognize something from a study guide or practice test—it may have been slightly changed for the exam.
	Skip around, if needed.	It's not necessary to start at the beginning and answer all questions in order. You may consider tackling shorter/easier sections first to lock in those points, then focus on more difficult areas.
	Keep a close eye on your time.	Remember that pace you briefly calculated right before the test? Check your time throughout the exam and do your best to stay on track.
Right after the test	Check over the entire test before submitting.	There are several reasons why you should double-check all your answers before turning in your test: • To look for any questions you might have missed • To make sure you followed directions correctly • To make sure you answered all questions completely • To check for any spelling/grammar errors (on written responses)

The Variety of Exam Questions: What to Expect and How to Approach Them

After much anticipation, the big moment has finally arrived. You're now sitting in front of the test and it's time to see if your hard work will pay off. What do you see? Specifically, what do the questions look like and how do you go about answering them correctly? We've covered in some detail how critical your preparation is in order to be successful on exams and also discussed some general test-taking strategies. However, there is another skill set you can develop that will also be important in determining that final grade. In this section, we'll look at the various types of questions you are likely to encounter in an exam setting and provide some guidance on how to approach them.

Here's a list of the five most common question types that occur on exams and specific strategies for how to answer each one effectively:

1. **Multiple Choice.** The "workhorse" of the common exam. If the test is not short answer or essay based, odds are most of the questions will be multiple choice.
    - ***Strategies:***
        - Read the question carefully and try to anticipate what the answer will be *before* you read the answer choices.
        - Read *all* answer choices before deciding on an answer.
        - Eliminate any answer choices you think are obviously wrong (if you can write on the test, you may even want to draw a line through these to focus in on the better options).
        - If two answer choices appear to be pretty much identical, they're probably both wrong.
        - Take note of information from other questions on the test. Sometimes a statement or answer from one question can tip you off to the answer on another.
2. **True/False.** Although you always have a 50/50 chance of getting them right, true/false questions can be tricky, and some students may even prefer multiple choice to them.
    - ***Strategies:***
        - Read these extremely carefully—it can be easy to get tripped up on the wording on this question type.
        - Look for absolute words such as *always* or *never* in the question—if you see one of these, the statement is more likely to be false.
        - Look for relative words such as *often*, *usually*, or *generally*—these are more likely to indicate that the statement is true.
        - If any part of the statement is false, the whole thing is false.

3. **Matching.** This question type is not as common, but here are a couple things to consider that can increase your odds of success.
   - ***Strategies:***
     - Make sure you understand the rules to the matching set. For example, can you use an answer item more than once? Are all options intended to be matched up?
     - Complete the matches you know first to narrow down your remaining options.
     - Mark off the options you've already used to focus on which ones you have left.
4. **Short Answer.** These can take a variety of forms, from just a couple of words to several sentences. Here are a couple tips to consider.
   - ***Strategies:***
     - Be sure you meet the length requirement and make your point, but don't write more than you need to—you could run the risk of stating something incorrect and getting counted off when it was not even necessary to write more than required.
     - Proofread your answer to double-check for grammatical errors and just to make sure it sounds logical and will make sense to your instructor.
5. **Essay.** Maybe the most dreaded form of test question but really nothing to fear if you are familiar with the topic. Follow these strategies to support your answer and show your instructor that you know what you're talking about.
   - ***Strategies:***
     - Read the essay prompt carefully to be sure you know what your instructor is asking and respond accordingly. For instance, are you being asked to compare two or more things? Are you taking one side or another of a particular argument? Are you supposed to generally describe your understanding of some topic and/or share your own thoughts or opinions on the subject?
     - Write as technically and professionally as possible, using terms specific to the subject as much as you can and avoiding slang.

Success Tip

You've probably heard phrases like "go with your gut" or "trust your instincts" applied to a number of life situations or decisions, right? This idea of trusting in yourself and your initial instinct also applies to test taking, particularly for multiple choice questions. When taking a test, pay attention to your thoughts that arise as you finish reading a question. Often, the first answer that strikes you as being correct (before you have a chance to overthink it) turns out to be the right one. I have personally observed many students over the years who changed their original correct answer to an incorrect second guess, as evidenced by the eraser marks on their paper or Scantron form. Now, if you realize for certain that your initial answer was incorrect, absolutely change it to something else. But, if you really get stuck on a question and can't decide which way to go, it's generally a good idea to trust your instincts and stick with your original answer.

- Try to organize your response logically by expressing your main idea then backing it up with as many supporting facts as possible.
- Once again, be sure you proofread your response for any writing errors and just to check for general readability (in other words, does it seem to flow naturally when you read it back to yourself?).

Activity 6.2 *Test-Taking Strategies: What Would You Do?*

Instructions: In the space provided or on a separate sheet of paper, describe how you would manage the situations below in four to six sentences, using what you've learned in the chapter.

1. Imagine you sit down to take a test. You are familiar with the content but were given absolutely no information on what the test would look like in terms of the length and types of questions on it. Describe some steps you would take to orient yourself before you mark a single answer.

2. Picture a different situation where you encounter a test composed of the following characteristics: a matching section (10 items worth 2 points apiece) with terms you're not 100% familiar with; a multiple-choice and true/false section (30 questions total, worth 2 points apiece) covering material you feel more comfortable with; one essay question that you feel pretty good about at the end worth 10 points. You have a 60-minute time limit. Describe how you would approach the sections of the test and what kind of pace you would try to keep. Provide a brief justification for your responses.

End-of-Chapter Questions

1. **Recall.** Define test anxiety. List a few techniques you can apply to reduce test anxiety. Name several reasons why you should double-check all answers before submitting a test. If you see two answer options on a multiple-choice test that are practically identical to one another, what does that probably say about these two options?

2. **Engage.** In a pair or small group of your classmates, discuss your experiences with college test taking up to this point. Which course subjects and/or question types do you find the most challenging? Which subjects and question types do you prefer and why? Discuss specific examples from your experiences and document your classmate's/classmates' responses in four to six sentences.

3. **Reflect.** In a 100-word response, discuss what you learned in the chapter related to test preparation and test-taking strategies. Which of these techniques do you think could help out the most and why?

4. **Create.** Using the content in this chapter, create the following test sections: one 5-question matching section, four true/false questions, four multiple-choice questions, and one essay question on any topic from the chapter. Afterward, make a key for each section you created. (Welcome to your instructor's world!)

References

North Shore Community College. (n.d.). *Test-taking strategies.* https://www.yumpu.com/en/document/read/38182603/test-taking-strategies-north-shore-community-college

Sawchuck, C. N. (2017, August 3). *Test anxiety: Can it be treated?* Mayo Clinic. https://www.mayoclinic.org/diseases-conditions/generalized-anxiety-disorder/expert-answers/test-anxiety/faq-20058195

Wachelka, D., & Katz, R. C. (1999). Reducing test anxiety and improving academic self-esteem in high school and college students with learning disabilities. *Journal of Behavior Therapy and Experimental Psychiatry, 30*(3), 191–198. https://doi.org/10.1016/S0005-7916(99)00024-5

Image Credits

IMG 6.1: Copyright © 2012 Depositphotos/lenanet.

CHAPTER 7

TMI (Too Much Information)

How to Recognize and Use Reliable Sources of Online Information

Image 7.1

Introduction

We live in an amazing time in history for many reasons, one being the entire world of information that exists at the tips of our fingers via the internet. The only problem with this situation is that much of the information out there on the Web is unreliable, biased, or untrue. Because a large part of the college experience is learning how to navigate, recognize, and utilize this information, it's important to develop your skills in online information literacy. In Chapter 7, we'll explore the following themes:

- Learning how to spot unreliable information online in its various forms in order to avoid being deceived by it
- Locating peer-reviewed research literature online by searching your college's online database collection and other sources
- Utilizing research literature sources in a paper or course assignment

Here's a brief summary of the main sections contained in Chapter 7: In "Is This Legit? Tips for Online Information Literacy," the student is exposed to various sources of unreliable online information and how to recognize it in Activity 7.1—Online Information Red Flag Scavenger Hunt. "Locating Research Literature Online" reviews several locations online where students can locate peer-reviewed research literature and includes Activity 7.2—Let's Find Some Research Literature! And finally, "Now What? How to Correctly Use Your Sources" presents the absolute basics of how to use research literature sources in a paper or assignment via in-text citation and includes the general format and an example for creating a reference list entry for a source.

Information is not knowledge.
—Albert Einstein

Is This Legit? Tips for Online Information Literacy

Ah, the internet. It's a wonderful thing, isn't it? A magical place of nearly limitless possibilities and practically endless amounts of information. Whatever you're into, odds are you can find it on the Web. Whether you're looking to fix that belt on your dryer, check the weather in Antarctica, or stream your favorite podcast or TV series, the internet has you covered. It's a place where you can see, meet, and even *be* just about anyone. You can learn a new language, pick up a new hobby, or even connect with people around the globe with interests similar to your own, no matter how obscure they may be. "*Wait, you're an ancient astronaut theorist, too?? No way!*" Like we said, folks, the possibilities are endless!

Okay, in all seriousness, the internet truly is a wonderful thing despite some of its drawbacks, including negative effects on time management and your self-esteem. It is an incredible resource that has completely revolutionized the way we learn and do research, and the amount of *good* information available online is simply amazing. But, on the other hand, it's no secret that the internet also contains an equally amazing amount of really *bad* information as well. With this in mind, the goal of this section is to provide some tips and advice on how to tell reliable, useful legit information sources from others that might be somewhat deceiving, extremely biased, or just flat out inaccurate.

The American Library Association defines **information literacy** as the ability to locate, evaluate, and effectively use information (American Library Association, 2021). So here we are looking at how to *evaluate* the credibility of your sources; the remaining sections will cover how to *locate* and *use* them effectively. And since the use of online media is now the dominant method for personal and academic purposes, this chapter will focus solely on analyzing and using digital sources of information.

Online Information Literacy: What to Look Out For

Learning how to evaluate the quality of online information has become an increasingly valuable skill in our technology-driven society. Even though many young people have grown up as digital natives and social media experts, this does not mean they have been taught how to spot unreliable information on the internet. For example, a report by Stanford University revealed that over 80% of students in their study could not tell the difference between a paid advertisement posing as a news story and an actual news story from a legitimate source (Wineburg et al., 2016). Since this issue has such a large potential impact on you as an individual as well as our society as a whole, let's take a closer look at how to spot (and avoid) bad information on the internet.

Here are a few warning signs, aka "red flags," that should help you locate and avoid questionable sources of information online.

Red Flags for Unreliable Online Content:

- **Social media.** Yes, here we are talking about social media yet again. But we all know what an integral part it plays in the way so many of us communicate and get our information these days, so it would be negligent to not mention it in this chapter. Once again, social media is not all bad, especially if used in a positive way. A recent study by the Pew Research Center found that many people actually appreciated the way social media introduced them to new ideas that may be educational or enrich their lives in some way (Smith et al., 2019). However, this same study found that many people regularly encountered false or misleading content on their platform, or—even worse—reported seeing information that made them feel divisive and negative toward other groups of people.

  Social media can be a viable space for keeping up with current events, pop culture, and even actual news related to politics or social issues; however, it's important to keep in mind that many individuals or groups use these sites as platforms to aggressively promote their own beliefs for personal or political gain. In doing so, these people may express their views and opinions as absolute fact (and most believe this to be true) in an attempt to manipulate or at least persuade you to think the same way as them. Clearly, in this type of post, you are not likely to get unbiased or reliable information. A good general rule to follow here is never believe anything you read on social media without question. Do a little of your own research before accepting any "fact" or statement as being true. Although some social media sites such as Facebook already have fact checking built in, it's never a bad idea to run any claim you read through an independent fact checking site to determine its accuracy. Several nonpartisan fact checking sites you can utilize include PolitiFact (https://www.politifact.com/), FactCheck.org (https://www.factcheck.org/), and Snopes (https://www.snopes.com/).

- **Misleading graphs.** If you look closely enough, you'll see that graphs on media sites are often deliberately made to exaggerate some kind of point that the news outlet is trying to make to fit or enhance their agenda. The big news media sites all do this to some degree, whether they lean to the left or the right, liberal or conservative. Obviously, they will manipulate the appearance of data or the data itself to make their argument or stance on an issue seem more compelling and believable to you, the consumer. With a little critical reading and knowing what to look for, you can learn to spot these graphs and avoid being tricked by this misleading tactic.

There are several common ways in which websites can achieve (or attempt to achieve) this kind of deception. One of these involves the vertical scale (or Y-axis) of the graph. The designers of the graph might make the values of this scale too large or too small. They may also leave certain numbers out, mislabel the graph, or not start the scale at zero. By not starting the vertical scale at zero, you can make a relatively small change in some value over time (interest rates, income levels, unemployment rates, etc.) appear to be larger or more dramatic than it really is. Additionally, they might have a big, bold headline designed to grab your attention, but upon closer inspection, a footnote in fine print will clarify what the graph is actually showing. The truth of the graphic illustration is usually never as shocking or controversial as the headline would have you believe.

- **Sponsored content.** Often, an advertiser (aka "sponsor") will pay a website to embed an advertisement within their site that appears to be a regular piece of content consistent with the general style of what would normally appear on the webpage. In a sense, the sponsored content ad is somewhat disguised to blend in with the website itself and be less noticeable or intrusive compared to a regular ad. Sponsored content is meant to appear credible and trustworthy as it is typically related to and placed among content that the viewer enjoys on a website they chose to visit.

  This may not be the most sinister form of misleading information; in fact, you may discover a product or program through sponsored content that you actually like and benefit from. Still, it's good to be able to spot this type of ad and know that someone paid to have it placed in front of you with the intention of getting your business. If you see a small note next to a website feature such as "partnered with," "powered by," or "sponsored by," you can be certain that the company name that follows directly after that note paid for the content you are seeing.

  Although it was not nearly as subtle in the beginning of its existence, sponsored content has been around for over 100 years (Santeralli, 2021). In the 1920s, radio stations began reaching out to companies to buy advertisements that would in turn help fund the programs on the radio (before the age of television, much of the radio programming consisted of fictional dramas, not unlike many of the popular television series of today). Proctor and Gamble was the first company to sign up and advertise their laundry detergent, Oxydol, on the radio. As it turned out, the marketing ploy was a big hit and the very first "soap operas" were born.

Activity 7.1 *Online Information Red Flag Scavenger Hunt*

Okay, now that we've identified three different types of red flags signaling unreliable online information, let's put our new knowledge into practice and sharpen our analytical skills in this area.

Instructions: Locate an example of each type of red flag listed below. In the space provided or on a separate sheet of paper, provide the web link to your findings and give a brief description of each one. Be sure

(Continued)

Activity 7.1 (*Continued*)

to specify how it is biased or deceiving and indicate what it was that tipped you off to the questionable content.

1. **Social Media.** Any social media platform is fine for this; just locate a biased or deceiving post or news story and follow the instructions above. If you don't have a social media account, try using YouTube *(youtube.com)* instead.

2. **Misleading Graphs.** Locate at least one misleading graph online and describe using the instructions above (hint: if you simply type "misleading graphs examples" into Google or another search engine, you're bound to find several to choose from).

3. **Sponsored Content.** Find an example of sponsored content anywhere online and describe using the instructions above.

Locating Research Literature Online

Now that we've learned a bit about online information literacy and how to recognize bad or misleading information online, let's look at this issue from a different angle and through a more academic lens. Recall that information literacy involves *locating*, *analyzing*, and *utilizing* credible sources of information. In this section, we'll cover how to locate legit, reliable information on the Web, specifically peer-reviewed, scientific research literature. This type of information is typically required in research papers or other assignments, and you are not likely to make it out of college without being required to use it at some point.

Although it may sound a little intimidating at first, research literature can be very interesting and relatively straightforward. The good news is that if you know where to look, it really is quite easy to find. All the major academic disciplines out there, from English to computer science to biology, have a rich body of research literature, with some studies going back 100 years or more. They also maintain a thriving culture of pushing the envelope with current, up-to-date research. Any cutting-edge scientific discovery or breakthrough in the social sciences will always appear in the research literature of its specific discipline to make it official. As we mentioned just a bit ago, these studies are **peer-reviewed**, meaning they are reviewed for accuracy by a panel of experts in their field before they are allowed to be published in a book or scientific journal. This process gives the information credibility as a reliable source, which is why research literature is often required for use in major assignments or in upper-level courses.

In this section, we will focus on two main sources for locating research literature online:

1. Your college library's online database collection
2. Publicly available online sources

Let's take a look at each of these in more detail, then follow up with another hands-on activity to gain some experience in utilizing both sources.

Your College Library's Online Database Collection

Any college in the United States that offers academic library services should have an electronic media collection available for its students and campus community. In fact, we are now seeing the amount of digital media provided by college libraries skyrocketing, whereas physical print collections are in decline (Cox, 2020). This trend, spurred on even further by COVID-19, is expected to continue in our technology driven, post-pandemic world. The wonderful thing about the online collection at your college library is that you can access digital materials at any time and from anywhere, as long as you have an internet connection. Various types of digital media (popular magazines, electronic books, videos, movies, etc.) may be available, but here we are mainly concerned with locating research literature that can be used in course-related papers and assignments. Although every college library collection will be accessed a little differently, let's look at some basic steps for getting to your online library services and learning how to use them.

Clearly, the best place to start when looking for your college library's online collection is the main website or homepage for your institution. If you don't see a link to library services, try using the search box or quick links area that most college websites now have. Note that you will almost certainly have to login with your student account information at some point to actually access these services, so be sure you have that information handy. It costs money for the college to subscribe to online books, journals, and other materials, so these things are generally not available for use by the general public.

Once you get into the online database collection, there will likely be various ways to search for the materials you need. Again, each system will be unique to the college, but here are a few general tips for navigating the online database collection search area:

- **Search by subject.** This is the best way to begin exploring your topic of interest to see what's out there. Simply type in a few key-words related to a research issue you want to explore, hit search, and see what comes up. You will likely need to revise or refine your search several times to find what you want, but this is a good place to start.

Success Tip

As we've said before, when in doubt, consult your student services professional! In this case, any staff member of your library or learning center should be able to help you locate and navigate the online data-base collection to find your research literature. Your course instructor can also help, but the folks in the library specialize in these services, so take advantage!

- **Search by journal.** Much of the research literature on any topic exists in peer-reviewed scientific journals. Your online library system may give you the option to browse or search by the journal title and may contain entire volumes in your field of interest. If you don't have a specific issue in mind, this can be a great way to get in touch with current studies going on in your field and see what interests you.
- **Search by author.** Once you find a study you like, it can be a good idea to search by the name (or names) of the author(s) to check for related studies by them on the same, or similar, topic. Of course, this method would not be very useful until you do become familiar with an author in your field.
- **Filter by "peer-reviewed."** Many search tools will have the option to filter results to include only peer-reviewed studies. This will eliminate any popular or opinion-based articles and leave you with only reliable research literature to work with—a very convenient feature, indeed!
- **Filter by date.** This can be a useful filter if you are wanting or needing only recent studies for an assignment. For instance, you can set this to return only studies published within the past three years or even less, if needed.

Hopefully, through some combination of the above techniques, you can successfully locate reliable research literature to satisfy requirements in your coursework or just to become informed in your major field in general. Keep in mind that learning to search for literature in your library's digital collection will be a skill that requires some practice (you will actually be getting some of that very soon). Don't be discouraged if it takes several tries to refine this skill to find the type of information you need—this is completely normal. But if you do get stuck, don't hesitate to reach out to your instructor for help or reach out to your library professionals as mentioned in the study tip, above.

Publicly Available Online Sources

The digital media collections at most colleges are truly remarkable resources. Most of them provide access to thousands of current studies, often as complete copies that can be downloaded for further use. Many of these articles would cost around $50 or more just for a single copy so we really should appreciate and take advantage of our college's collection. However, you should also be aware that there are some online sources of research literature out there on the Web that are completely free and available to the public, regardless of college or university affiliation. Let's take just a few minutes to examine a couple of these sources so you can add them to your toolkit.

- **Free online research databases.** There are multiple database sites out there that are completely open access or at least partly free (contain some free articles and others that must be paid for). Many of these partly free databases can be filtered to include "full-text only," which eliminates any content that costs money. Still others may require you to register in order to access the database, but the registration is totally free. All of these provide at least some of their content for free, and if you add them all together there are many thousands of current, peer-reviewed studies in research literature available for download by anyone. Several online research databases to explore that are at least partly free include the Education Resources Information Center, aka ERIC (https://eric.ed.gov/); ScienceOpen (https://www.scienceopen.com/); Directory of Open Access Journals (https://doaj.org/); and PubMed (https://www.ncbi.nlm.nih.gov/pubmed/).

- **Google Scholar.** Now, in general, the best way to locate research literature is *not* to simply "google it." However, Google Scholar is a little different from its more famous cousin. Google Scholar (https://scholar.google.com) can be a very useful tool for finding what you need. Because it is such a powerful and sophisticated search engine, Google Scholar can sometimes be the most efficient way to search an extremely broad array of research literature from across all disciplines. Many times, it may provide links to some of the open access databases like the ones we just mentioned.

  One drawback is Google Scholar does not provide a full-text only filter option, so many of the links it provides (especially for more recent articles) lead you to a site that requires payment to access the study you need. However, it will generally take you to at least an abstract (summary of the study) and bibliographical information including the publication date, author(s), and the journal in which it appeared. Here's a little pro tip: write the article information down, then go back and search in your college library's online database. With the specifics of the article plugged into your search, many times you'll be able to locate the study for free at your college rather than paying for access on another site. In other words, you can use Google Scholar as a powerful tool to identify interesting research studies, then take advantage of your college library to download free copies of them.

Activity 7.2 *Let's Find Some Research Literature! Yeah!*

Similar to Activity 7.1, let's put our newfound knowledge into practice and actually locate and briefly describe a research study utilizing our college library's online database collection.

Instructions: Login to your college library's online database collection and use the search tool to locate at least one peer-reviewed research study in an academic field that interests you (preferably related to your major, if you've chosen one at this point). Since they are very common in academic writing, let's locate a journal article as your research study. Be sure and use some of the search and filter functions described earlier in this section and reach out to your instructor or a library staff member if you need assistance with logging in or performing your search.

In the space provided below or on a separate sheet of paper, briefly describe which keywords you used for your search and any filters you applied. Finally, write a brief summary of the article and provide the name of the study and its author(s), the date it was published, and the name of the journal in which it appeared.

Now What? How to Correctly Use Your Sources

All right, now that we've had a little practice at locating peer-reviewed research literature, the final step in this chapter is learning how to properly use it in a paper or assignment. Once you learn the basics and stick to them, this is not terribly difficult to do, especially with a little bit of practice. Let's go over these basics and then apply them in some very simple examples.

First off, by **source**, we are referring to the actual research study (usually a journal article or book) you are using in a paper. The whole point of using research literature is to present information from experts in the field in order to validate a point you are making or support your argument with reliable, peer-reviewed data. When you use information from a study (aka source) in this way within one of your sentences in a paper, this is referred to as citing your source. When you cite a source within a sentence, this is called an **in-text citation**. At the very end of a paper, you give a full description of the study as a **reference list entry**. To wrap up this chapter, let's take a quick look at how to use an in-text citation and make a reference list entry.

In-Text Citations

These are much easier to understand with a simple example or two. Actually, if you look throughout this book, including in this chapter, you'll notice many examples of us using in-text citations to support a claim and identity the source of the information being stated. In-text citations are fairly easy to spot once you know what they look like.

There are actually two types of in-text citations. Parenthetical citations appear in parentheses and include the author of the article or research study followed by a comma and then the date of publication (American Psychological Association, 2020). Did you see it? There it was! Note that the author may be a person's last name (or multiple last names for multiple authors) or the name of an organization. In a narrative citation, you use the author's name in the sentence (outside of parentheses) and only put the publication date itself in parentheses, usually right after the author's name. We'll take a quick look at both methods very soon.

Just to note, there are actually several different styles created and managed by different organizations (such as the American Psychological Association, or APA) for using citations and references in writing. Since it is the predominant style used in social and natural sciences, we are using APA style in this book and in this section. Other styles include MLA (by the Modern Language Association) and Chicago Manual of Style citation formats.

Okay, let's take a quick look at two simple examples of how to use in-text citations in a sentence. For simplicity, we will not be using direct quotes from a source, as this would also require a page number included in the parentheses. This is consistent with APA style, which advises against overusing direct quotes in your writing. It's generally better to **paraphrase** what the author said—this simply means to put the information from the literature source in your own words. In this fictional scenario, let's say a study by Terry McKenna published in 2012 found that the majority of participants in the study who spent more time in nature reported greater levels of happiness and lower stress levels. If you were writing a paper in support of spending time outdoors, here's how you could use this source in a sentence to support your argument in either style of APA in-text citation:

Parenthetical citation example: A recent study found that individuals who spend more time in nature tend to be happier and experience lower levels of stress in their lives (McKenna, 2012).

Narrative citation example: A recent study by McKenna (2012) found that individuals who spend more time in nature tend to be happier and experience lower levels of stress in their lives.

See how it works? Not so bad, right? One more thing to note is what to do if the study has multiple authors.

- If the study has two authors, you list both with an ampersand (the "&" symbol) between the two last names like this: (McKenna & Sheldrake, 2012).
- If there are three or more authors, you list only the primary author's name followed by "et al." (which is just Latin for "and others"), then a comma and the publication date: (McKenna et al., 2012).

Note that in the reference list entry at the end, you would list all authors for a work; you just don't include them all in the in-text citation within the body of the paper.

Reference List Entries

Finally, we are going to briefly cover the format for listing your study at the very end of your paper in the references section. There are many types of sources that can be cited in a paper and listed in the references (journal articles, books, online news stories, etc.), but to keep it simple, we are going to stick with the format for a journal article in this section.

Here's an example of the basic format for a journal article reference list entry. Note that the font (italics and capitalization) and spacing have to be exact in order for it to be correct.

Reference list entry example (fictional journal article):

McKenna, T. K. (2012). The effects of time spent in nature on happiness and stress levels. *Journal of Natural Studies, 34*(7), 12–24.

Let's quickly break down the elements of the reference entry and point out a few details to note. Here are the elements in the order of their appearance and in the same basic format as above:

Last Name, First initial. Middle initial. (publication date). Title of article. *Title of Journal, journal volume* (journal issue), page range of article in the journal.

Here are a few things to note about the general format of the reference entry:

- Every element is separated by either a comma or period and a single space except for the journal volume and journal issue, which have no space between them.
- The title of the article is in regular font and only the first word is capitalized.

- The title of the journal is in italics and every word is capitalized (except for smaller words such as "of" or "the").
- The journal volume number is in italics but goes straight into the journal issue number, which is not in italics.
- The comma following the journal title is roman, not italics.
- The page range numerals are separated by an *en* dash, not a hyphen.
- One final thing to note is that all elements may not be present in every article. For instance, the author may not have a middle initial and the journal may not have an issue number. If either is the case, simply leave that element out.

We hope you've enjoyed this crash course on how to locate research literature online and use it in a paper! Or, at the very least, learned something from it. You may want to bookmark this last section, as it could come in handy for future use in actual course assignments. For further guidance on how to cite and reference all types of literature and media, check out the free online writing lab at Purdue University (https://owl.purdue.edu/owl/research_and_citation/apa_style/apa_formatting_and_style_guide/general_format.html).

And also, be sure to check with your own college library! It may provide useful materials and services related to this topic. At the end of the day, remember to not get overwhelmed. This stuff can get very technical, but there are always people and resources out there to help you navigate any issues that arise along your journey. Don't be afraid to use them; after all, this is a learning experience.

End-of-Chapter Questions

1. **Recall.** Define the term information literacy. What is a good general rule regarding any information you read on social media? List several nonpartisan fact-checking sites you can use to verify information you read online. Describe what it means for a research study to be peer-reviewed and why this is important.
2. **Engage.** In a pair or small group of your classmates, discuss your experiences locating research literature in Activity 7.2. Document your classmates' responses in four to six sentences and be sure to mention any search tips that may have come up in your conversation.
3. **Reflect.** In a 100-word response, discuss why it may be harmful for us, personally and as a society, to be frequently exposed to extremely biased and agenda-driven information on social media.
4. **Create.** Using the research literature journal article you located in Activity 7.2, craft a sentence with an in-text citation (parenthetical or narrative—writer's choice) to make a point you'd like to express and list your journal article, reference entry list style, using the chapter information and/or online resources.

References

American Library Association. (2021). *Information literacy.* https://literacy.ala.org/information-literacy/

American Psychological Association. (2020). *Publication manual of the American Psychological Association* (7th ed.). Author. https://doi.org/10.1037/0000165-000

Cox, C. (2020, June 5). *Changed, changed utterly.* Inside Higher Ed. https://www.insidehighered.com/views/2020/06/05/academic-libraries-will-change-significant-ways-result-pandemic-opinion

Santeralli, E. (2021, January 30). *Sponsored content: What you need to know (and 9 examples!).* ActiveCampaign.com. https://www.activecampaign.com/blog/sponsored-content

Smith, A., Silver, L., Johnson, C., & Jiang, J. (2019, May 13). *Publics in emerging economies worry social media sow division, even as they offer new chances for political engagement.* Pew Research Center. https://www.pewresearch.org/internet/2019/05/13/users-say-they-regularly-encounter-false-and-misleading-content-on-social-media-but-also-new-ideas/

Wineburg, S., McGrew, S., Breakstone, J., & Ortega, T. (2016). *Evaluating information: The cornerstone of civic online reasoning.* Stanford Digital Repository. http://purl.stanford.edu/fv751yt5934

Image Credits

IMG 7.1: Copyright © 2012 Depositphotos/Wavebreakmedia.

CHAPTER 8

Sailing On

Finishing Strong and Preparing for a Meaningful Career

Image 8.1

Introduction

Wow, last chapter already! We've covered a lot of ground on various topics and truly hope you've picked up a number of mindset and practical strategies to help you succeed in your community college experience. Now let's dive in one more time and talk about an extremely important part of your initial higher education journey: the conclusion. Specifically, your graduation, possible transfer, and preparing for your career beyond formal education. In Chapter 8, we'll explore the following themes:

- Preparing for graduation, including tips for staying on your academic pathway and the general steps for applying for graduation

- Transferring to the university and several factors to consider that may affect your decision on where to attend
- Preparing for your career—your life beyond the college classroom

Here's a brief summary of the main sections contained in Chapter 8: In "Cue the Celebration! Preparing for Graduation," we'll look at ways to stay on an efficient academic pathway, present a general checklist for the graduation process, and look closely at your own academic pathway in Activity 8.1—Exploring Your Pathway. Next, "Leveling Up: Transferring to the University" reviews several key factors to consider that may influence your decision on where to transfer. "Your Next Life: Career Preparation" presents the opportunity for students to learn more about their prospective career path in Activity 8.1—Exploring Your Chosen Career. Finally, in "Bon Voyage," the authors express a final well wishing to the student, leaving them with a reference list of "take home" points from the entire text in Table 8.1.

Sail away from the safe harbor. Catch the trade winds in your sails.
Explore. Dream. Discover.

—Mark Twain

Cue the Celebration! Preparing for Graduation

Although most of you are probably at the very beginning of your academic career, it's never too early to start thinking of about a major milestone in your life: your first college graduation! Recall in the very first chapter of the book we talked about the value of beginning with the end in mind. You can use this as fuel to motivate you toward your goal. Also, be aware that this event can sneak up on you sooner than you think, so it's good to be mentally prepared. Especially if you are able to attend college full time, you'll see that the two to three years it takes to complete your degree program will fly by. Before you know it, you'll be walking—no, *strutting*—across that stage to shake your college president's hand and receive that incredibly valuable piece of paper that you worked so hard for. Smile for the camera!

As we just mentioned, it's beneficial to keep graduation in mind for motivation and a positive mindset. In addition, from a practical standpoint there are things you need to be aware of to make sure you finish your degree and cross that finish line as soon as possible. In this section, we're going to look at the road to graduation, from your academic pathway to the process of applying for graduation, to get you onto the next phase of your journey where your future awaits.

The Academic Pathway: Your Highway to Successful Completion

Every certificate or degree program at your college has at least a degree plan to follow, and many institutions now have more specific academic pathways in place. A **degree plan** is simply a list of all the options for the courses required for your degree program, including the total number of credit hours. This type of plan may also suggest which courses could be taken from one semester from the next. Even if this is your first semester in college, if you have a chosen major, you've probably at least glanced over your degree plan already and may even have some vision for what you plan on taking in the next semester or two.

A slightly more detailed version of the standard degree plan is the academic pathway. An **academic pathway** is a well-defined sequence of specific courses to take each semester toward degree completion. In essence, these pathways are more structured versions of the degree plan designed to make your path to completion clear cut and more efficient. This can save you time and money by helping you get to graduation sooner than you may have otherwise. Academic pathways are intended to build knowledge and skills to support higher academic achievement and often include "stackable" certificates, which provide easy on and off ramps along the way to degree completion. If your program has an academic pathway, it is highly advisable that you stay on it. And, once again, if you can attend school full-time, you are more likely to successfully complete your program, and you will definitely save yourself time and money in the process. Keep in mind that for every extra semester you attend, you are not only paying tuition for the class or classes, you are also paying all the fees required just for being enrolled.

Academic pathways are gaining traction and becoming more popular as calls for efficiency and accountability in higher education continue to grow (Blagg et al., 2021). However, even if your institution does not yet have formal pathways in place, there are still actions you can take to create your own pathway and stay on it for a speedy completion.

Here are several steps you can take to stay on your own academic pathway:

1. **Study your degree plan.** Carefully study your plan and get familiar with all the courses you will need to take. Take note of which ones are absolutely required, and where there are options, look into these and decide which ones you'd prefer.

2. **Strategize a sequence for taking your courses.** Attempt to plan out exactly which courses you will take every semester until you graduate (consider summer semesters and mini sessions to speed up the process). Check past course schedules or consult with your advisor to make sure the classes you need are usually offered in the terms you have planned for them. Even if you have to adjust this plan a little down the road, it still helps to have one in place.

3. **Estimate your time to completion.** Note the total length of the certificate or degree program and plan on how long it will take you to finish. This will make it seem more concrete and should motivate you to keep going!

4. **Talk to your advisor throughout the process.** As you know by now, your academic advisor is your resident expert for getting you in the classes you need when you need them. Consult with them at least once a semester to make sure you are on track.

Applying for Graduation

The first thing you need to know about graduation is that you must apply for graduation. The college is not likely to notify you when you complete your degree requirements. They are extremely unlikely to just automatically award your degree once you finish all your courses. All this means is that it's generally up to you to keep track of how close you are to completing, especially toward the end of your program. By keeping up with this, you can insure your opportunity to graduate as soon as possible and get on to the next level of your academic or professional life! Going through the graduation process is generally not very difficult, especially compared to all the tough courses you've taken to get to that point. As soon as you think you are eligible to graduate in the upcoming ceremony (graduation—aka "commencement"—ceremonies usually occur in spring, summer, and fall), consult the steps to follow, which are generally provided by your admissions department. The process will likely look like the following checklist.

Typical Graduation Process Checklist:

- **Contact your dean or program director.** They can confirm that you have in fact met all the program requirements and are eligible to graduate.
- **Apply for graduation.** Pay close attention to the deadline for application!
- **Attend graduation rehearsal.** You don't want to look lost during your big moment on stage!
- **Attend graduation.** You've earned your right to walk across that stage so take advantage of it. This accomplishment and your memory of this ceremony will stick with you for the rest of your life.
- **Receive your diploma.** Your actual diploma is usually mailed to you a short time after graduation. Frame that baby and hang it with pride!

Activity 8.1 *Exploring Your Pathway*

Instructions: In the space provided or on a separate sheet of paper, provide a brief response for each item below related to your academic pathway at your institution.

1. Do a little research on your certificate or degree program using your college website. If you don't have a specific major chosen yet, explore one of the top programs you are considering. Does it appear to be a traditional degree plan or is it a more detailed academic pathway? Explain your answer in one or two sentences.

2. Considering how many courses you are able to take in an average semester, estimate how long it will take you to finish your program. What is the earliest term (semester and year) you believe you would be able to graduate?

Leveling Up: Transferring to the University

If you're reading this right now, there's a very good chance you are planning on (or at least considering) transferring to a four-year institution at some point to complete a bachelor's degree and possibly beyond. This can be a possibility for you, whether you're in an academic or technical major. Choosing a transfer institution is a big decision that will largely shape the next step in your education and your career. Here are three broad factors to consider when deciding on where to go next.

The Location

Or, as the old saying goes: "location, location, location." Just like in real estate, the location of your transfer university is extremely important and should be carefully considered. Here are some questions to ask yourself regarding this issue:

- **Is it in my state of residence?** This is a big one as it can dramatically affect the cost of tuition. Out-of-state students can easily pay two to three times as much as in-state residents, possibly even more. If you're not covered by grants or scholarships, this can be a very big deal.
- **What are my options for housing?** Are there affordable options for student housing (aka dorms) or reasonable apartments or rental properties near campus? Is it somewhere you would feel safe and comfortable living, working, studying, et cetera? Most universities do have student-friendly housing nearby, but you will want to do your best to minimize your commute, so you don't end up paying too much for gas or risk being late to your classes.
- **What's the general cost of living like?** Another financial concern to consider is the general cost of living in the city you are moving to. Make sure your budget will allow you adequate food security and the ability to purchase basic necessities (and maybe even have a little fun every now and then).
- **Will I have family help or support?** Depending on your background or personality, this might be a factor to consider. For some students, having some kind of family connection or close friends in the area could be reassuring and possibly affect your decision to attend one university over another. On the other hand, you could also view this opportunity as a chance to move away from your support system and experience something completely different for a change. Depending on your goals and

Success Tip

College is a personal journey and an adventure all unto itself. Having family support can be beneficial and may even be necessary in some cases. But, moving somewhere totally new and unfamiliar and making it on your own can also be an amazing experience—one that leads to personal growth and expands your sense of individuality and self-reliance. It seems that life often rewards us for courageous acts that put us firmly outside of our comfort zone, and college can provide multiple opportunities for this. Your university transfer experience may be the right time make a big leap of faith into unknown territory. You might be surprised to see where it leads you.

personal preferences, this can be a very positive, rewarding experience and a path that's well worth considering.

Institutional Characteristics

In addition to where the university is located, it's also important to research what the college itself is all about. Usually, the university's homepage will provide enough information to at least give you a pretty good idea about its fundamental characteristics.

Key factors such as the size of the institution, its history (how long it's been around), whether it's a public or private institution, if it's a for-profit institution or not, and their admissions standards should be readily apparent without too much searching on their website. While you're at it, make sure the college is accredited. This information should be considered a key determining factor and should also be readily available. An **accredited college** is one that's approved and regularly audited for quality by a panel of experts from an organization called a regional accreditation body (Fernandez, 2020). Accreditation is important for transferring credits to other colleges and for the college to be eligible to disburse federal financial aid to its students.

If you dig a little deeper on the website, you can likely find some student success data for the institution. This may include some of the standard metrics we discussed in Chapter 1, such as retention and graduation rates, and also may contain interesting facts like the average class size, job placement rates, and average time to completion. All of these data points can help you get a feel for the quality of the institution and your odds for success should you decide to attend there. If you don't see very much information on their site, or just want to dig deeper, every college in the country submits a variety of success data to the U.S. Department of Education; this data is publicly available (https://nces.ed.gov/ipeds/).

Of course, you will want to get familiar with the academic programs the university offers, particularly the one that pertains to your major. This may be what draws you to the college in the first place, but if you're looking at multiple schools be sure to look closely at the departmental websites for each to get a general feel and see which one seems more established or appeals to you on a personal level. These sites should have information on the courses they offer and the instructors who teach them. You may even find success data specific to the department, and you should definitely see contact information for the department chair or program director. If you're seriously considering attending the program, you should reach out to them for more information or even to arrange a tour of the department (if feasible). Most academic programs are in a constant state of active recruitment and should be more than happy to provide information to a prospective transfer student.

Another factor to consider would be the campus culture. What traditions exist at the school? What kinds of clubs, organizations, or sports teams do they have on campus? What is their mascot and what are their colors? It's good to get a feel for the general makeup of the student body and the diversity it may represent. Read their mission. What do their core values seem to be and do they align with your own? Although the quality of their academic programs may ultimately have a greater impact on your future, keep in mind that essentially you will be living in this environment for at least the next two years. Feeling comfortable on campus and having a sense of community or belonging can increase your quality of life during that time and may even improve your chances for academic success.

The Cost of Attendance

One more factor to briefly discuss is the cost of attending the colleges you're considering. If you feel very strongly about a particular university program, it may be worth pursuing even if it's a little more expensive than others. But the cost of attendance, combined with the prospect of receiving scholarships or other forms of financial aid, may turn out to be a deciding factor when choosing between two or more colleges.

We mentioned the cost of living in a particular area, but what about the cost of tuition and fees? A couple of the key characteristics we just went over come into play here. Note that a private institution is generally more expensive than a public one, and for-profit colleges tend to charge more than their nonprofit counterparts. While we're on the subject, you should be extremely cautious in general when considering attending a for-profit college. These institutions have a history of producing higher loan debt and lower job prospects for students compared to nonprofits. Recent estimates show that for-profit schools only enroll about 10% of the U.S. college student population, yet they account for about *half* of all student loan defaults (Shiro & Reeves, 2021). In addition, many of these institutions were forced to close their doors, following the impact of Obama-era legislation, due to poor performance. As we said: proceed with caution.

Your Next Life: Career Preparation

When the smoke clears and you earn your last degree, the next phase of your life begins: your *career*. Notice we didn't say *job*. All of the hard work, time, and money that the college experience demands will truly be worth it if you follow your heart and pursue a meaningful career path for the right reasons. The funny thing is, once you hang up your student cap and go to work, a whole different world of learning opens up to you. It really never ends, but the "studying" and the tests you encounter will usually look quite different.

Whether you are here at the community college to knock out a certificate or associate's degree in two years or less and go straight into your career or you're planning on a graduate degree and many more years of formal education, the time to begin researching your ideal career is *now*. So what are we waiting for? Let's spend the rest of this section doing a deep dive into your chosen career, or at least one of your top prospects for a career path at this point.

Activity 8.2 *Exploring Your Chosen Career*

Instructions: In the space provided or on a separate sheet of paper, provide a brief response for each item below related to your top career choice at this moment.

1. What is the minimum education required for this career and how many years of study does this involve?

(Continued)

Activity 8.2 *(Continued)*

2. What types of institutions (community college, university, technical, on-the-job training, etc.) do you need to attend in order to get into this career?

3. What types of skills, talents, or personality traits are needed to succeed in this career?

4. Describe any skills or personal traits you currently have that would benefit you in this career.

5. Describe any skills or personal traits you would need to develop in order to be successful.

6. What is the beginning wage or salary to expect for this career?

7. What is the median or average wage and how much could you expect to earn at the maximum end of the salary range?

8. Describe any health or retirement benefits that are typically associated with this career.

9. Describe the nature of sick leave and vacation time typical of this career.

10. Are there any health or safety concerns associated with this career?

11. What is the current outlook for employment in the field and is the demand for this career projected to grow in the future?

(Continued)

Activity 8.2 (*Continued*)

12. Describe a typical workday for this career, including the hours you'd be working.

13. What do you think would be the most enjoyable or rewarding part of this career for you?

14. What do you think will be the most challenging aspect of this career?

Bon Voyage

Well, my friend, you made it! We've reached the end of our journey together, but your road is likely just beginning. It's been an absolute privilege sharing what we've learned over many years in the community college environment, and anything that you can take from this book to inform and enrich your experience moving forward would be an honor of the highest degree. It's why we set out to write this book in the first place and what keeps us going day after day, semester after semester, year after year.

We hope you may view this text as a sort of field guide, or survival guide, and use it to help navigate future elements of your college experience as many of the concepts should continue to apply. With that in mind, we'd like to leave you with a short summary table of the key "take home" points from each chapter, with references on where to find them. Bookmark this table; may it serve you well on the road ahead. In parting, we want to wish you the best possible community college experience and a truly rewarding career beyond! Believe in yourself, stay positive, follow what drives you, and be sure to help others. The rest will all fall into place.

Bon Voyage!

Table 8.1. TAKE HOME POINTS FROM EACH CHAPTER WITH REFERENCE LOCATIONS ON WHERE TO FIND THEM.

Chapter	Take Home Points	Section	Page Numbers
1	Stay positive, stay motivated, stay present Begin with the end in mind	Mastering Your Mindset	3
		Beginning With the End in Mind	11
2	Questions to ask your advisor Local and federal financial aid options	First Contacts: Admissions and Advising	16
	Student loan borrower's guidelines	Financial Aid Demystified	19

(*Continued*)

Table 8.1 (*Continued*)

Chapter	Take Home Points	Section	Page Numbers
3	Good choices lead to positive outcomes; bad choices lead to negative results and more stress	A Day in the Life	29
	Five key time management practices	Time Management 101: 5 Key Practices	36
4	The Golden Rule: treating others with respect	Cultural Understanding and the Golden Rule	42
	Study group optimization techniques	Engaging With Peers	43
	Instructor email etiquette	Communicating With Instructors	47
5	Top three reasons to attend class	Why Attendance Matters	52
	Five key study practices	Study Tips and Techniques: 5 Key Practices	55
6	Techniques for reducing test anxiety	Be Prepared: Test Preparation Techniques	60
	Strategies for the five most common test question types	The Variety of Exam Questions: What to Expect and How to Approach Them	66
7	Definition of *information literacy* Red flags for unreliable online content	Is This Legit? Tips for Online Information Literacy	71
	How to use in-text citations and reference list entries	Now What? How to Correctly Use Your Sources	78
8	Staying on your academic pathway Graduation checklist	Cue the Celebration! Preparing for Your Graduation	83
	Follow your heart and pursue a meaningful career	Your Next Life: Career Preparation	88

End-of-Chapter Questions

1. **Recall.** Define an academic pathway and briefly describe some of its benefits. What does it mean for a college to be accredited and why is this important? Why should you be extremely cautious when considering enrollment in a for-profit institution?

2. **Engage.** Pair up with a classmate or form a small group one last time and discuss your plans for completing college and starting your career. Be sure to talk about how far you will need to go with your education (i.e., associate's, bachelor's, graduate degree), which career field you are planning to enter, and how long you think it will take to get there. Document your classmate's/classmates' responses in four to six sentences.

3. **Reflect.** In a 100-word response, write out your thoughts in a final reflection of the textbook as a whole (you do not need to discuss every chapter). Which chapter was your favorite and why? Describe how any lessons or strategies covered within the text could benefit you on your academic journey.

4. **Create.** What if you had to describe this textbook (or the course) to a friend who was about to take it? In your own words, summarize what you think is the main idea of this text in two to four sentences, then describe what you liked about it and how you think it could be improved (what else would you like to see in a book like this?). Be honest and objective in your assessment. Thank you for sharing in this journey, and best of luck on your own path!

References

Blagg, K., Blom, E., Kelchen, R., & Chien, C. (2021, February). *The feasibility of program-level accountability in higher education.* Urban Institute. https://www.urban.org/sites/default/files/publication/103634/the-feasibility-of-program-level-accountability-in-higher-education.pdf

Fernandez, M. A. (2020, May 19). *What is an "accredited" college? Why is being "accredited" important?* College Raptor. https://www.collegeraptor.com/find-colleges/articles/questions-answers/accredited-college-accredited-important/

Shiro, A., & Reeves, R. V. (2021, January 12). *The for-profit college system is broken and the Biden administration needs to fix it.* Brookings. https://www.brookings.edu/blog/how-we-rise/2021/01/12/the-for-profit-college-system-is-broken-and-the-biden-administration-needs-to-fix-it/

Image Credits

IMG 8.1: Copyright © 2014 Depositphotos/Rawpixel.

CPSIA information can be obtained
at www.ICGtesting.com
Printed in the USA
BVHW021333160323
660602BV00002B/11